"Invite *The Gift of Recovery* to accompany your journey home to yourself. You'll meet no better guides to support your day-to-day recovery goals than authors Williams and Kraft. Their exercises, meditations, affirmations, and self-inquiry questions are grounded in their non-judging and compassionate understanding of addiction and recovery. This book will help you be kinder to yourself, even as you deepen your self-awareness and commitment to sobriety."

—**Amy Weintraub,** author of *Yoga for Depression* and
Yoga Skills for Therapists, and founder of the LifeForce
Yoga Healing Institute

"*The Gift of Recovery* is a well-crafted, beautiful illustration of the power of mindfulness in healing from addiction. From compelling examples to memorable metaphors, the authors use a conversational approach to appeal to their audience and simplify the often-confusing jargon of psychotherapy. Short chapters, organized as 'gifts,' compel the reader to redefine their view of the recovery process. Mindful exercises and affirmations help the reader transform thoughts into action. Audiences will find it helpful to use independently or as an adjunct to their work in therapy. Comprehensive, masterful, and approachable, Williams and Kraft have done it again, bringing together the best evidence-based concepts to addiction recovery in this one absolutely essential guide."

—**Gina M. Bongiorno, LMFT,** manager of the co-occurring
substance and eating disorder program at the University
of California, San Diego's Eating Disorder Clinic; and
adjunct faculty member at the University of San Diego

"In today's world focused on apps and technology, this 'gift' brings it back to the fundamental instruments needed to help keep my clients focused and being present. As a clinician, I am inspired to use this as a parallel process and enhance my skill set."

—**Jason R. Allison, SAP, ICADC, LAADC**, licensed addiction professional and cofounder of National Therapeutic Alliance

"Sustaining recovery is a complex process—it involves learning skills that will help you get through tough moments, and figuring out how and when to implement them when you need them most. Even more than making healthy choices in the moment, sustaining recovery also comes to life when you learn to be kind, curious, and even forgiving of yourself along the way. *The Gift of Recovery* strikes that beautiful balance. Williams and Kraft teach practical steps while fostering a spirit of compassion that will facilitate you making choices that honor your values, needs, and goals in an effort to live beyond addiction."

—**Rachel Hershenberg, PhD**, assistant professor of psychiatry and behavioral sciences at Emory University, and author of *Activating Happiness*

"*The Gift of Recovery* presents a precious path into a new way of living for people recovering from any kind of addiction (or just struggling with life). Williams and Kraft were able to capture every scenario and situation that a person in recovery might face, and give them tools that could literally save their lives. They intimately know the world of addiction and its struggles as well as the way to recovery and its joys. I highly recommend this book."

—**Lynn Rossy, PhD**, author of *The Mindfulness-Based Eating Solution*, and executive director of Tasting Mindfulness, LLC

"If recovery is what you're looking for, look right here. ... Without question, *The Gift of Recovery* has become an integral part of my mindfulness practice and is already weaving its way into programming throughout my three organizations. Highly recommended for all those looking to say goodbye to addiction and hello to serenity."

—Christopher Bennett, CADC-II, CIP, BRI-I,
chief executive officer and founder, Chris Bennett Interventions; cofounder of the Chris Buro Foundation; and founder of Encore Recovery Solutions

"This is one of the few books I've read that zeros in on recovery principles I believe are essential in achieving long-term recovery. It is an easy read that identifies issues that lead to relapse, and provides practical anecdotes using mindful meditation techniques. A simple read of this valuable recovery material will be helpful in itself, but practicing the mindful meditation techniques will put learning into practice and optimize one's comfort level in recovery."

—Bob Tyler, BA, LAADC, CADC II, owner of Bob Tyler Recovery Services; CAADAC past president and CCAPP founding board member; LMU Extension faculty in the alcohol and drug studies program; author of *Enough Already!*; and producer of the DVD, *Craving and Relapse*

"Kind, wise, and eminently practical, *The Gift of Recovery* provides powerful skills and practices to help transform the habits, urges, and thought patterns that keep you hooked in unhealthy behaviors. Rebecca E. Williams and Julie S. Kraft offer a generous toolbox of mindfulness skills to help you live your life with joy and freedom. A true gift!"

—**Hugh Byrne, PhD**, senior teacher with the Insight Meditation Community of Washington, cofounder of the Mindfulness Training Institute of Washington, and author of *The Here-and-Now Habit*

"This is the gift that keeps on giving. In *The Gift of Recovery*, Rebecca Williams and Julie Kraft provide the reader with fifty-two gifts to guide them through their recovery from addiction. I believe this book is a gift for everyone who struggles with leaving behind unhelpful and unhealthy habitual behaviors. Rebecca and Julie provide great mindfulness skills and multiple affirmations for each day of the week. They make the reader feel that they are with the intelligent and compassionate companions that we all need as we face the challenges on our journey to a healthier, joyful life. This is the best mindfulness book I've read in a long time. Give yourself this gift. You deserve it!"

—**Michelle Skeen, PsyD**, author of *Love Me, Don't Leave Me*; and host of *Relationships 2.0*

"*The Gift of Recovery* will be a valuable guide for anyone wanting to incorporate mindfulness into your path of recovery from addiction."

—**Tim Desmond, LMFT**, author of *Self-Compassion in Psychotherapy* and *The Self-Compassion Skills Workbook*

the
gift of
recovery

52 Mindful Ways to
Live Joyfully Beyond Addiction

REBECCA E. WILLIAMS, PhD
JULIE S. KRAFT, MA, LMFT

New Harbinger Publications, Inc.

Publisher's Note

This publication is designed to provide accurate and authoritative information in regard to the subject matter covered. It is sold with the understanding that the publisher is not engaged in rendering psychological, financial, legal, or other professional services. If expert assistance or counseling is needed, the services of a competent professional should be sought.

The names and events in this book are fictional. Any likeness to real people is coincidental.

Distributed in Canada by Raincoast Books

Copyright © 2018 by Rebecca E. Williams and Julie S. Kraft
New Harbinger Publications, Inc.
5674 Shattuck Avenue
Oakland, CA 94609
www.newharbinger.com

Cover design by Amy Shoup

Acquired by Camille Hayes

Edited by Brady Kahn

Library of Congress Cataloging-in-Publication Data on file

20   19   18

10   9   8   7   6   5   4   3   2   1   First Printing

For Michael,
Thank you for this most amazing adventure

—Rebecca

For Jennifer Salyer: we are forever grateful that you came into our lives.
For Sarah Nichter, the best friend on planet earth.
And for my Markley boys:
I wouldn't ride this roller coaster with anybody else!

—Julie

*Tell me, what is it you
plan to do with your one wild and
precious life?*

—Mary Oliver

Contents

Acknowledgments   ix

Introduction   1

Section 1: Beginning Your Mindful Recovery

1   Welcome to a New World   8

2   Understanding Meditation   12

3   A Mindful Good-bye to Addiction   16

4   Mastering the Breath   20

5   Sitting Still   24

Section 2: Emotions

6   Getting Comfortable with Moods   28

7   Gratitude for Feelings   32

8   Soothing Anger   36

9   Releasing Fear   40

10   Accepting Everyday Frustration   44

Section 3: Especially Strong Emotions

11   What to Do with Especially Strong Feelings   50

12   When Emotions Get Stuck   54

13   Honoring and Releasing Old Ways of Coping   58

14   Letting Pain Be Pain, Not Suffering   62

15   Self-Compassion   67

Section 4: Thoughts

16   Minding Your Mind   72

17   Changing Your Thoughts   76

18   Tricky Addiction Thinking   80

19   Tricky Recovery Thinking   85

20   The Inner Bully   89

21   Positive Thinking   93

22   Racing Thoughts   97

Section 5: Cravings and Triggers

23   Awareness of Triggers   102

24   Coping with Cravings   107

25   Reconnecting to Cues   111

26   Urge Surfing   115

Section 6: Mindfulness Skills and Stress Relief

27   Changing Your Perspective on Stress   120

28   Progressive Muscle Relaxation   123

29   Removing Unnecessary Stress   127

30   Practicing Acceptance   131

31   Decluttering Your Space   134

Section 7: Cultivating Relationships

32	Creating a Support System (and Using It)	140
33	Relationships That Don't Work	144
34	Dating and Intimacy	148
35	Telling Others About Your Recovery	152

Section 8: Improving Relationships

36	Communicating Well	158
37	Resolving Conflict Mindfully	162
38	Resentment and Forgiveness	167
39	Other People's Feelings	171

Section 9: Bonding with Your Body

40	Love and Respect for Your Body	176
41	Prioritizing Sleep	179
42	Mindful Eating	183
43	Mindful Movement	187
44	Yoga and Recovery	190

Section 10: Values and Self-Worth

45	Knowing Your Worth	196
46	Discovering What You Value	200
47	Being Money Mindful	204
48	Reconnecting to Work	208

Section 11: Sustaining Joyful Recovery

49 Recovering Each Day   212

50 Playful Recovery   215

51 Special Occasions   219

52 Maintaining Recovery Over Time   223

    Resources for the Road   227

    References   235

Acknowledgments

A heartfelt thank you goes out to the many clients, veterans, and family members who have shared their struggles and successes with us over the years. Whether you know it or not, your commitment to your recovery and mental health helps others connect to a meaningful recovery too! We are especially grateful to our students and colleagues at the VA San Diego Healthcare System and the University of San Diego, School of Leadership and Education Sciences for clearing the path towards understanding, kindness, and compassion. Truly inspiring.

We would also like to express our gratitude to the skillful team at New Harbinger: Jesse Burson, Caleb Beckwith, Vicraj Gill, Amy Shoup, Fiona Hannigan, Candice Jacobus, Jennye Garibaldi, Brady Kahn, and Camille Hayes. You all really know how to make writers sparkle.

Introduction

*It may be that when we no longer know what to do, we have
come to our real work and that when we no longer know
which way to go, we have begun our real journey.*

—Wendell Berry

Have you ever had the feeling that you were on this recovery journey alone? Of course, the noise in your head is a constant companion, but not always helpful if you are having a less than perfect day. Feeling out of control, stressed, angry, anxious, fearful, sad, lazy, and, yes, lonely, is a normal part of recovery. If these are normal feelings, then why do your days feel like such a struggle?

What do you want first, the good news or the bad news? The good news is that you are on the right track; you have everything you need to have a magnificent life without addiction. Now for the bad news. You must put some quality work in to reap the rewards of recovery; no one is going to hand you anything for free. You need a plan, a consistent approach, to cultivate your mental, emotional, physical, and spiritual well-being. Just like a garden that needs to have sunshine, food, and water on a regular basis, your recovery will grow and thrive when you begin to nourish it with a steady supply of mindfulness. So, let's uncover what mindfulness is and how it may be your companion in recovery.

What Is Mindfulness Anyway?

You may have come across the word "mindful" or "mindfulness" recently in lots of self-help books, training courses, and DVDs. *Mindfulness*, put simply, is a popular psychological approach to personal healing in a stressed-out world. The idea of mindfulness began with the Buddhists, who integrated it into their meditation practice. Mindfulness was popularized in the West by Jon Kabat-Zinn (2013), who started using mindfulness skills to help decrease the anxiety of cancer patients. Kabat-Zinn created the mindfulness-based stress reduction program with great success at the University of Massachusetts Medical School over thirty-five years ago.

Mindfulness focuses on bringing your attention to the present moment, the here and now. It's a way of teaching the brain to become aware of what's happening inside and outside the body. Many research studies have shown that practicing mindfulness is correlated with well-being. Practicing mindfulness has been shown to reduce symptoms of depression and anxiety in adults and children (Gotlink et al. 2015). More recently, mindfulness-based practices have been used in the treatment of and recovery from drug and alcohol addiction (Williams and Kraft 2012). These practices can help manage addictive urges and cravings, which may decrease relapses.

Recovery from drug and alcohol abuse works best when there is a plan with lots of support along the way. Recovery from other troubling behaviors like gambling, overspending, overeating, sexual acting-out behavior, and overworking also requires your full attention in moment-to-moment awareness for the success that you are hoping for. The idea here is to begin to let go of stressful and damaging thoughts and feelings and reconnect with yourself and your life in a calm and accepting way. This book will provide you with many mindful practices and exercises that you can carry with you to support your recovery from addictive behaviors.

Who This Book Can Help

Now, you know that you need some type of plan to balance your life in recovery. The question is, what does this plan look like and are you really going to follow it? You've seen plans fall by the wayside many times before. How is this plan going to be any different? Well, this little book is designed exactly for the days when you are having doubt, struggle, conflict, and generally a bad attitude. It is also useful when you are feeling pretty good, your day is going well, and you would like it to stay that way. Reminders on how to stay the course in your recovery make sense.

This little book is intended for people who are just beginning recovery and need a boost to make it through the day or the week. It is also aimed at those who have sustained long-term sobriety and need a refresher on soothing and centering themselves. Our book is meant for all those who have wrestled with addictive behaviors. While we often apply the word "use" or "using" to refer to addictive behavior, the skills in this book will be as helpful to those recovering from gambling, food, or sex addictions as they are to those recovering from alcoholism and drug addiction. Think of your use as whatever behavior you are striving to change in your life.

How to Get the Most from This Book

If you have read and put into practice the skills from our workbook *The Mindfulness Workbook for Addiction: A Guide to Coping with the Grief, Stress, and Anger That Trigger Addictive Behaviors* (Williams and Kraft 2012), then you have set the groundwork for your recovery. This book continues where that workbook leaves off. You can think of this book as your pocket coach, offering ways to bring you back into the practice of recovery and recommit to your long-term success. Here's how to get the most from this book.

Take your time. This book is designed to provide you with one thought and one mindful practice at a time. You have the option of reviewing the concepts and practicing one skill per week for an entire year, or you can choose when you need to touch base with your recovery and pick up this pocket coach as a refresher whenever you like. You might want to skip ahead to a section and choose another mindfulness practice to try. You may find that certain areas speak to you the most and may want to circle back to other areas later. You are in charge of how you benefit from this book. The gift of a healthy and joyful recovery is in your hands.

Activate the daily affirmations. Each mindfulness topic comes with seven affirmations. An *affirmation* is a positive statement that strengthens you by helping you believe in the possibility of reaching your goal. These affirmations are designed to be used each day of the week, so you can stay on track with your recovery. How you activate these affirmations is up to you. We recommend that you say them out loud throughout the day to connect with your intention of a mindful recovery. We also recommend, if you have a smartphone, that you type the daily affirmation into your phone each morning as a reminder to say it three to five times per day. You can activate the affirmations differently, however. The key is to use them. The seven affirmations are the cornerstone to change your brain and your way of thinking.

You can download a printable copy of each set of affirmations to carry with you throughout the week at the website for this book: http://www.newharbinger.com/40705. This page also contains audio for a selection of affirmations.

Practice the exercises. The word "practice" or "meditation" should not be scary. Anyone can benefit from training the mind to slow down. The idea is to practice noticing what thoughts and feelings arise in you without reacting to those thoughts and feelings. The meditation practices in this pocket coach are designed to encourage your mind to relax and experience a moment of peace. These and the other suggested exercises in this book set the stage for you to experience self-compassion, patience, forgiveness, hope, and well-being. We

4

could all use more of these experiences! Audio for several guided meditations as they appear in this book is available at http://www .newharbinger.com/40705. (See the very back of this book for more details.)

Keep a journal. A journal is your sacred place to jot down reactions to the meditation skills that are presented here. You can add some of your own ideas. You can expand on the skills we have outlined for you or create more skills just for yourself. You can take note of which skills work best for you and when you use these skills: at work, at home, with family, when you are alone, when difficult feelings arise, or when things are going well. This will help you customize the skills to your specific needs, and the journal can become a reminder of when to practice a certain skill.

Talk to a counselor or therapist. This companion book is devised to remind you of how to soothe your mind in recovery. Meeting on a regular basis with a professional counselor allows you to explore and expand your understanding of life without addictive behaviors. This book can be the added ingredient to your individual therapy, to your group therapy, to your recovery meetings, or to your aftercare program.

So it's time to take charge of your joyful recovery, and use this little book as a gentle reminder to stay the course. We are excited to join you on your mindfulness journey!

Beginning Your Mindful Recovery

1

Welcome to a New World

Wherever you are is the entry point.

—Kabir

When I (Julie) was a child, I loved to hang upside down. I would flop myself over the side of the couch and absorb the world this way. Feet in the air, head nearly touching the floor, I would examine every nook and cranny of the room. All of it was now suddenly unfamiliar. I imagined what it would be like to walk on the ceiling and who I would be if I lived there. I had found a whole new world. And all I had to do was turn myself over.

We all have our set ways of doing things. So much of what we do, so much of how we move through the world, becomes automatic. We get set in our ways. Our experiences become routine. Fuzzy and flat. A lot of times we don't like how we are living or we don't like how we feel. Our usual ways of doing things aren't getting us what we want. Yet we try them again and again. And again. You have probably heard the definition of insanity as doing the same thing repeatedly and expecting a different result. If that's true, most of us are ready for the straitjacket.

This is never truer than when we are addicted.

It seems to be the very nature of addiction to repeat painful, harmful, heartbreaking behaviors over and over again. The addicted life becomes habitual. Stopping by the same liquor store on the way home. Visiting the same casino. Lining up your paraphernalia in some specific routine way. Even if you saw the consequences coming, you were so stuck in your addiction that you simply couldn't do things differently. You continued to step in the very same footprints that led you right over a cliff. It's not your fault. It's a compulsion. In addiction, you were driven to act in the same old ways.

Taking a Step Back

Let's have just the quickest science lesson here. Brain science, that is. Because of cutting-edge technologies, we know more about addiction than we ever have before; we get to peek into the human brain with new scans and watch what it's up to. Understanding how the brain influences addiction may not be everything in recovery, but it is a valuable piece. It's empowering to have this kind of insight. So here are some of the things that science tells us.

First, human beings, like other mammals, have a built-in reward system in the brain, called the *reward pathway*. When we do normal things like eat or have sex, the natural chemical dopamine surges in our brains and makes us feel good. Good enough to send the message *I should keep doing that.*

Drugs, alcohol, and other addictive behaviors hijack your reward pathway, however. They create levels of dopamine in the brain that are off the charts compared with what happens with normal pleasurable behaviors. This is how the addiction takes over the most natural, basic survival system for any mammal, and *I should keep doing that* is still the message, no matter the cost.

So, here you have it. Here is the picture of addiction. The addiction steals this natural, healthy reward system and tells you that you need this substance or behavior to survive. Meanwhile, people around you, and probably you yourself, think it's crazy for you to keep doing this destructive behavior, especially when the consequences are getting more and more severe, and it would be easy to feel hopelessly stuck. However, that hopeless feeling is just another trick of the mind. Recovery happens! It is happening right now, in this moment. It is happening with every sober breath.

Through mindfulness, you can do things differently. What was automatic can become flexible. What was limited and small can open up for you. Mindfulness practice means having *curiosity* about your experience. It means allowing things to be what they are, without judgment. It is looking at the world with new eyes. It is staying present with what is, rather than dwelling hopelessly in what was or what might be. There is a calmness to this process. There is also a sense of wonder. There are choices. There is pleasure in the simple things.

If repeating the same thing over and over again and expecting a new result is insanity, trying out new behaviors and being open-minded about their result is finding clarity. Is this possible? Could what was dull become shiny again? Could what frightened you make you curious? Make you brave? Could the things you turned away from begin to call to you, to invite you into something new?

What happens when you flip yourself over? That is what this book and this process are all about. You will be learning skills, ideas, and techniques designed to change the way you experience the world and the way you move through it. There is so much waiting for you in your mindful recovery. Go ahead and turn yourself head over heels, one moment at a time.

Exercise: Noticing Your Automatic Behaviors

Committing to your mindful recovery is the ultimate gift to yourself. As a way of committing to this process, choose an activity that you do automatically and make a conscious choice to do it differently. You might spend a few minutes looking at your room upside down. You might try narrating every detail of your drive to work (*I turn the steering wheel gently to the right; it feels smooth and cold in my hands. I exit the highway behind a red car that is moving slowly...*) or describe each step of tying your shoelaces, as if you were teaching it to a child. You could try drawing or painting or pouring milk into a bowl of cereal with your opposite hand. Have some fun. Notice how the experience becomes strange and new, bringing you back to the present moment.

Affirmations for Stepping into Mindful Recovery

We recommend you say these affirmations out loud throughout the day to connect with your intention of a mindful recovery. We also recommend you type one affirmation into your smartphone each morning as a reminder to use it three to five times daily. You can download a printable copy of these affirmations at the website for this book: http://www.newharbinger.com/40705.

Monday: *I stay present, in the here and now, and thrive in my recovery.*

Tuesday: *I am willing to turn myself over and see the world in a whole new way.*

Wednesday: *I can understand my cravings and urges; I don't have to act on them.*

Thursday: *Addiction is the result of a substance or a behavior hijacking my healthy brain. I can make new choices and take my life back.*

Friday: *I don't have to follow the same old patterns that led me astray. I choose to move in a new direction.*

Saturday: *All things are possible for me today.*

Sunday: *I choose to recover mindfully.*

2

Understanding Meditation

You are lost the instant you know what the result will be.

—Juan Gris

You are probably familiar with the Serenity Prayer: "God, grant me the serenity to accept the things I cannot change, the courage to change the things I can, and the wisdom to know the difference." Recovery from addiction has a lot to do with this sense of balance.

Meditation is where you will find the courage to change the things you can change and the serenity to accept what you can't. (And, yes, the wisdom to know the difference, too.)

Basically, meditation is a practice that quiets the mind. But sometimes meditation is not what you expect. It will be helpful to know what to expect, realistically, from your meditation practice.

Meditation isn't easy. It may sound simple to sit still and be present, but it's a lot harder than it sounds! Instead of being in the present, you may find yourself thinking about the past or planning for the future. Buddha himself probably contemplated his to-do list during meditation from time to time. The truth is that no amount of skill or practice is going to stop you from being human. Embrace this truth by simply noticing when your attention has moved away from the present moment and gently inviting it back. That's one way to dwell in the here and now. (And it really does get easier with practice.)

You may bump into your inner bully. We will talk more about your inner bully later, but suffice it to say that a nasty, self-critical voice may show up while you are meditating. Doubts about whether meditation is really worthwhile, whether it can help you in your recovery, or whether you are capable of practicing it may arise. Hang in there. There is no such thing as being perfect when it comes to meditation. All you can ask of yourself is to *show up*. Give yourself the space and time to meditate, and connect with what happens next.

Meditation doesn't always feel good. If you expect instant peace and contentment from your meditation practice, you may be disappointed. It's true that meditation will often help you relax and tune in to the present moment in a way that feels really wonderful. But sometimes it won't. Sometimes meditating can actually feel stressful. You may experience restlessness or agitation. Please know that there's nothing wrong with you or your practice if this happens. It may be unpleasant, but it's really okay. Notice what is happening for you, and trust that all feelings are temporary.

All experiences are created equal. This is a tough one to swallow. It's natural to favor pleasant experiences over unpleasant ones. You may decide you are "meditating well" if you feel relaxed and are able to focus (Bowen, Chawla, and Marlatt 2010). You might think unhelpful thoughts, such as *This isn't working* or *I can't do this*, when you are easily distracted or stressed. This is all part of the process! Accept that distraction is just one experience; the ability to focus is another. During one meditation, you may notice tension in your body, and in another you may feel at ease. Do your best to let go and allow your experience to be what it is.

Through meditation, you will learn to greet all the experiences of your recovery with open-mindedness, compassion, and peace. That kind of serenity is certainly worth the work! Audio for the next meditation exercise is available at http://www.newharbinger.com/40705.

Exercise: Greeting Your Experience

Find a quiet place where you have the opportunity to concentrate and to feel peaceful. Because meditation can make you sleepy, and you want to stay awake for your practice, it is best to sit up instead of lying down. Make yourself comfortable and decide to sit still for several minutes. You may start with five minutes, or ten, or maybe thirty if you have been meditating for a while. You might want to set an alarm so that you don't feel the need to watch the clock.

Close your eyes if you feel comfortable that way, or let your gaze fall gently to the floor. Turn your attention to your breath. Allow your breathing to become slow, deep, and even. (If this is challenging, please refer to chapter 4 on mastering the breath.)

Now, notice your attention. Your attention is beautiful, and powerful, and pure. It is a beam of radiant white light. See the beam and how it moves where you ask it to. You can focus that beam of light wherever you choose.

As you sit in the here and now, shine your attention on each sensation that arises. Perhaps it is an itch on your neck, a twinge of hunger in your stomach, the feeling of calm, or the noise of anxious thoughts. There is no need to change the sensation. *There is nothing here that needs to be fixed.* Instead, bring your attention to the sensation. Shine your light on the sensation, sit with it for a time, explore it with curiosity, and then shift the light away. Perhaps you will revisit the same sensation again and again, shining the light on one itch, for example, and then turning the light elsewhere and returning to the itch again. You are noticing what happens when you attend to the sensation and what happens when you turn your attention away.

If your attention seems to scatter, that's just fine. You can notice where it wandered to and gently bring it back. You can refocus it into this powerful beam of light as many times as you need to. You are greeting each experience that arises here today. The warm light of your attention is welcoming all that arises in the present moment.

Affirmations for Understanding Meditation

We recommend you say these affirmations out loud throughout the day to connect with your intention of a mindful recovery. We also recommend you type one affirmation into your smartphone each morning as a reminder to use it three to five times daily. You can download a printable copy of these affirmations at the website for this book: http://www.newharbinger.com/40705.

Monday: *I am open to all that arises in my meditation today.*

Tuesday: *I can tolerate uncomfortable feelings, and I know they are temporary.*

Wednesday: *I greet my experiences in life and in meditation.*

Thursday: *My attention is beautiful and powerful and pure.*

Friday: *I choose to show up for my meditations; I am present for whatever arises.*

Saturday: *There is no such thing as being perfect in meditation. I accept my practice as it is today.*

Sunday: *I welcome every sensation as it is meant to be.*

3

A Mindful Good-bye to Addiction

*The moment you accept what troubles
you've been given, the door will open.*

—**Rumi**

As the song says, breaking up is hard to do. Nostalgia tugs at your heart-strings. Memories creep into your mind or pop up in your dreams. You know you'll be better off; you know it's time to move on. Things have been looking pretty bleak, and the pain far outweighs the pleasure. But still, breaking up with your addiction—really saying good-bye—can be confusing and emotional. As therapists, we have heard our clients refer to their addictive behavior as "my lover," "my partner," or "my best friend." Addiction is a relationship, after all. And to be honest, you two were close. You spent holidays together, vacationed together, and saw each other regularly. You turned to your addiction in the hard times, when you needed someone to lean on. You turned to your addiction in the good times, too. You couldn't imagine celebrating without it.

We don't mean to glorify your addiction. There is absolutely no doubt that a clean and sober life, free from addiction, is a hundred times better than life as an addict. But it's important to be honest about how you feel. In mindfulness practice, you approach your experience with openness, honesty, curiosity, and interest. You don't have to judge your experience, but you do have to take a clear look at it. And whether you are new to recovery or have been away from your addiction for many years, there is bound to be some *ambivalence.* That's fancy talk for feeling more than one way about something.

It is natural to feel conflicted about saying good-bye. You may find yourself reminiscing about the good times, when you felt so happy together. Or you may find yourself eager to shut the door on this relationship for good, only to find that it sends love letters every once in a while, trying to win you back. (We will talk more about cravings and triggers, and how to handle these, in the pages ahead.)

So what do you do with all these thoughts and feelings? Once you know it is right to end this relationship, how do you say good-bye?

Feel it; don't fear it. It is perfectly normal to experience the loss of your addiction as a loss, and just like with any other loss, you will have a period of grief. It is natural and healthy to grieve. If you find yourself very resistant to your grief, ask yourself what grieving means to you. Do you take grieving your loss as a sign of impending relapse? It is not. Acknowledging your feelings about saying good-bye is different from not really being able to say good-bye or idealizing what you've lost. Or are you afraid you won't be able to tolerate certain feelings? Coping with difficult feelings is not easy, but ignoring them doesn't really help. Many chapters ahead offer new techniques for dealing with difficult feelings.

Use other good-byes as your road map. As you look at other times you have closed the door on a relationship, what lessons arise from your experience? Did you linger longer than you wish you had? Did you pull the covers over your head and stay in bed for days? Did you end up getting sucked back in instead of really saying good-bye? Do you tend toward self-blame, obsessing about the past, and not really letting yourself let go? What about times you have said good-bye gracefully? How did you do it? How did that feel? Take these lessons for what they are and carry them forward. You have a wealth of knowledge and experience within you.

Connect with others. It's easy to get into self-pity when you think you're the only one who has ever suffered a loss. Start a conversation with people you trust about times they have had to say good-bye to people, places, or things. If this feels a bit awkward, try telling them it's an experiment or a project, something you are trying to learn more about. Most people really don't mind telling you their stories if you are truly listening. Ask what feelings arose for them and how they moved through their good-byes. Don't talk; just listen. Bring your mindful curiosity and open-mindedness to these conversations. See what unfolds.

Accept the greater truth that loss, grief, and endings are all a natural part of life. Experiences of saying good-bye are powerful. They can bring out the best and the worst in people. While grief may seem like a stuck place, it is often the catalyst for something amazing. Losses are stepping-stones. Where will this good-bye take you? Leaving this relationship with your addiction is truly an act of courage. It is a bold step toward freedom. Step confidently, and keep striding!

Exercise: Writing the Good-bye Letter

Write a good-bye letter to your addiction. Tell it exactly why you have decided to part ways. Give as many examples as you can think of; tell it how it's done you wrong. Tell it how you will miss it. Explain why you are sure your life will be better without it. Read over your letter a few times, and then tuck it away for later. You can bring it out to read at any point. You can even take a picture of your letter and keep it on your phone, to have with you all the time. Read it during the rough times and the good times.

After you write your good-bye letter, put pen to paper and write a *hello letter*. This second letter is your opportunity to greet all the things you would like to add to your life now. The hello letter is about enhancing the current good things in your life and adding in some goals and dreams you would like to focus on this year. Don't leave anything out.

Remember that both the good-bye letter and the hello letter represent your ability to connect with yourself now and to chart your course going forward.

Affirmations for a Mindful Good-bye to Addiction

We recommend you say these affirmations out loud throughout the day to connect with your intention of a mindful recovery. We also recommend you type one affirmation into your smartphone each morning as a reminder to use it three to five times daily. You can download a printable copy of these affirmations at the website for this book: http://www .newharbinger.com/40705.

Monday: *I close the door on my addiction and step forward into a better life.*

Tuesday: *I say good-bye to my addiction and say hello to joyful recovery.*

Wednesday: *I am curious about all the feelings that arise as I let go of addiction, both the comfortable and the uncomfortable.*

Thursday: *I am beginning to understand that endings are beginnings.*

Friday: *I open my heart to what comes next.*

Saturday: *My intention is to be aware of my feelings about endings and to notice without judgment.*

Sunday: *Today I meet the day with a fresh start in my recovery.*

4

Mastering the Breath

You don't have to see the whole staircase, just take the first step.

—Martin Luther King, Jr.

"I tried every drug there is," Kristen says. "I tried maxing out my credit cards on clothes. I tried dating lots of men. I tried eating nothing but cake. I tried anything I could think of to make life feel more livable for me. I can't believe the answer was really as simple as a pure, deep breath."

Your breath is incredible. Have you noticed? It is keeping you alive: the inhale, the exhale, the gentle pause between. Your breath is an amazing asset in your recovery from addiction. But if you are like most people, when it is most important to use this skill, you simply forget it exists. It is so common to forget your breath! And instead, you search frantically for an answer, for a fix outside of yourself. Turn inward instead. Turn to your breath.

Lonely? Your breath is always there for you. It is your companion and your ally. You are never, ever without it. Your breath is in constant conversation with the world around you. Consider how you are breathing in tandem with the plant life around you, how truly connected you are to all living things. In reality, you are never alone. Your breath is here to remind you of that.

Overwhelmed? Your breath will bring you back to this moment. Whatever is demanding your attention is on hold for this one breath. Your breath asks nothing of you. It will be there for you whether you pay attention or not. You don't need to try. You don't need to work. But if you do give it some attention, it will give you so much more. With each breath, you are restored; you are energized. You have the time and space for this breath; it is yours.

Uncertain? Your breath will give you an answer. It is your gateway to that wise inner voice. It can take you beyond the chatter of the mind. As you focus on your breath, your thoughts slow down, and what was fuzzy comes into focus. There is clarity here, awaiting you with each breath.

Stressed? In your breath, you will find your center. You will uncover your calm. With your breath, you will release any tension from the body. You can feel yourself letting go as you exhale. There is a greater sense of peace and well-being available to you in this moment, all because of your breath.

Learning to tap into the power of your breath is an essential part of your mindful recovery from addiction. Remember to breathe!

Exercise 1: Noticing the Breath

To tap into the power of your breath, you must first *notice* it. That is the mindful way. This exercise will guide you into a deeper connection with your breath.

Find a quiet place where you can be free from distractions for at least five minutes. This is the time to turn off your phone and put it away in a drawer. Acknowledge that you are giving yourself the gift of this undivided time.

Allow yourself to sit comfortably, preferably with your feet planted on the floor and your hands resting easily in your lap. If it feels right, close your eyes, or simply gaze gently toward the floor. Take this moment to enjoy a good, deep breath. Let the air move into your body slowly, purposefully. As you breathe, notice any sensations in your nose, in your throat. Gently fill your lungs down to your belly, feeling the belly rise naturally. Breathe to your center. Let this breath fill you up. Realize that you are being sustained. You are getting what you need. Feel the belly fall. Let the air move slowly out of you, back into the world around you.

Continue breathing this way for a few minutes, focusing on each breath. How do you feel? Maybe you feel just the same. Or quite possibly that one breath, that brief moment, changed something for you. It may be subtle or profound, but it happens.

Continue to bring your attention back to your breath, noticing the sensations of the breath and breathing deeply, several times each day, whether it is for one breath only or for several minutes.

Audio for the next meditation exercise is available at http://www .newharbinger.com/40705.

Exercise 2: Meditation for Soothing with the Breath

Now that you have noticed your breath, it is time to strengthen your skills for using the breath to soothe, relax, and bolster you. Sit quietly as you did before, and this time gift yourself with ten minutes of undistracted time. Make yourself comfortable, close your eyes, and bring your attention to your breath. Pay attention to breathing from your belly rather than from your chest. Breathing only from the chest is shallow breathing and will not give you the same level of calm. Take the time to slow and deepen your breath.

As you breathe, focus specifically on what you want to draw in and what you want to send out. You can name what you want, then focus on the word, expanding it slowly on the inhale and the exhale. For example, if you choose to inhale peace, focus your attention on the word *peeeee-ace* as you breathe in. As you exhale stress, imagine the out-breath carrying the stress out of your body and letting it float easily away. Use the following list of soothing words to guide your meditation:

Inhale peace, exhale stress.

Inhale calm, exhale tension.

Inhale self-compassion, exhale judgment.

Inhale acceptance, exhale resistance.

Inhale joy, exhale sorrow.

22

Inhale trust, exhale fear.

Inhale clarity, exhale uncertainty.

Inhale gratitude, exhale worry.

Now, begin to slowly count as you breathe, inhaling for five slow beats and exhaling for five slow beats. Allow your inhale and your exhale to become balanced, smooth, and slow. Continue this counting for five slow breaths.

Notice what arises as you do this exercise, and leave room for your experience to be different with every practice. Learn from each of your moment-to-moment experiences and allow them to be what they are.

Affirmations for Mastering the Breath

We recommend you say these affirmations out loud throughout the day to connect with your intention of a mindful recovery. We also recommend you type one affirmation into your smartphone each morning as a reminder to use it three to five times daily. You can download a printable copy of these affirmations at the website for this book: http://www.newharbinger.com/40705.

Monday: *When anxious or stressed, I return to my breath.*

Tuesday: *My inner wisdom is waiting for me in this breath.*

Wednesday: *I exhale tension. I breathe in peace.*

Thursday: *Today I will remember my breath.*

Friday: *Everything I truly need is contained in this one breath.*

Saturday: *No matter what happens, I can pause and breathe.*

Sunday: *There is always enough time for this breath.*

5

Sitting Still

Real silence means there is actually nowhere else for the mind to go.

—**Anandamayi Ma**

If you were anything like me (Rebecca) growing up, you were the know-it-all. Always the first to answer the teacher's questions, sometimes answering before the teacher even finished her question. And so smug when you got the answer right, thinking to yourself, *That was so easy.* Maybe you were the type of kid who fidgeted in the chair, always antsy for the next activity. Always volunteering to be the snack monitor, the closet monitor, the put-the-toys-away monitor, the anything monitor. Always moving around. Let's face it, nap time was a joke. Did they really think taking a break was going to get you anywhere? Nap time was for the little kids, not you. What if you missed out on something? Maybe you still feel this way: you don't want to miss out on anything, ever. They have a word for that nowadays: FOMO. Fear of missing out.

Recovery from addictive behavior is a lot like being that fidgety kid in school. The mind attaches to so many things at once, unable to calm down or slow down. Using substances was a way to keep the bouncy brain in check. But as the substances wear off, there you are again with the noise of the next activity, the next thought, the next feeling, and the next answer to problems not yet experienced. How do you slow your mind down but not totally check out? Is it okay to take a little break?

Well, you are in luck. This gift of sitting still is really a gift of *permission.* We are giving you permission to slow down, permission even to stop for a few minutes. Here is how it works.

First, thank your brain for being so curious and so interested in everything around you and so ready to give out lots and lots of answers! The mind is designed to think, to give suggestions, to snoop, to ponder. Your mind is extremely active. Whether it's watching a reality television show, reading the latest post on Facebook, looking up a new recipe, or solving your friend's relationship problem, your brain is constantly onto the next attention-grabbing activity. There is never a dull moment. In fact, you might even pride yourself on multitasking. If you have a habit of texting while walking, returning e-mails during a business meeting, or talking on the phone while driving, consider this your wake-up call. Multitasking, the art of doing many things at the same time, has been shown to decrease your productivity. Doing too many things at once puts your brain into overload. In recovery, the idea is to reclaim your brain, not to overtax it.

Second, let your brain know that you are going to be going together on a minivacation. When was the last time you took a vacation with your recovering self? This time you will not need to pack anything for the trip. Leave everything exactly where it is. Everything? Yes, leave everything. You already have what you need to make this an enjoyable vacation. This vacation is something special; it will require you to sit still for five to ten minutes each day for a whole week. Are you ready?

Exercise: Sitting-Still Meditation

Find a comfortable quiet space. You can sit on a straight-backed chair with both your feet on the floor. You can sit on a cushion on the floor. Or you can lie down facing up on the floor with your legs slightly apart and your arms by your side, palms facing up. Any of these positions will do; the only goal is to *be still* for a few minutes. At first, it will feel awkward. You may have an immediate tendency to want to get up and continue what you were doing before. You may want to check your cellphone (you have permission to turn your phone off for this exercise). You may want to scratch an imaginary itch. We suggest that you notice that thought along with the millions of other thoughts that come into your mind. Noticing without reacting to the thoughts will bring you back to that place of stillness. Notice the thoughts, and return to focus on your breathing. Just the simple inhale and exhale. You may notice a whole host of feelings come bubbling up. Frustration, resentment, boredom, confusion, maybe even joy. Notice these feelings and allow them to move through without reacting to them or getting in their way. Notice the feelings, and return your focus to your breathing. Just the simple inhale and exhale. Remember this minivacation has been designed with you in mind.

Affirmations for Sitting Still

We recommend you say these affirmations out loud throughout the day to connect with your intention of a mindful recovery. We also recommend you type one affirmation into your smartphone each morning as a reminder to use it three to five times daily. You can download a printable copy of these affirmations at the website for this book: http://www .newharbinger.com/40705.

Monday: *I give myself permission to unplug so that I can unwind.*

Tuesday: *There is value to being quiet for a few moments.*

Wednesday: *Sitting still allows my mind to rest.*

Thursday: *Today I will find a few quiet moments for myself.*

Friday: *Stillness brings me back to meaningful recovery.*

Saturday: *My intention today is to notice when I am rushing around and to slow myself down.*

Sunday: *Being quiet always improves my mood.*

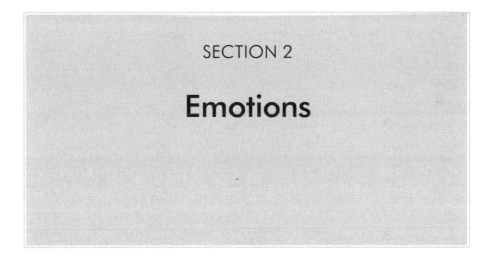

SECTION 2

Emotions

6

Getting Comfortable with Moods

*The ability to observe without evaluating
is the highest form of intelligence.*

—Jiddu Krishnamurti

"When I first got sober," Joe says, "I felt so bad for feeling bad. I thought a bad mood meant I must be doing something wrong in my recovery. Wasn't I supposed to feel great now? Wasn't I supposed to be grateful for my recovery? And it didn't help that when I got down, all my sober friends were quick to point out what step I should be working or something else I should do differently. Sometimes working on that step or doing that thing really did help. And I was feeling better, most of the time. And I was really grateful to be recovering. But you know what? Recovering or not, I'm human. I've got feelings, and sometimes I'm just in a bad mood."

Like it or not, feelings happen. Moods hit. Moods swing. This is especially true in early recovery. It is safe to say that addiction has a lot to do with feelings: avoiding feelings, soothing them, not knowing what to do with them, or maybe having a way to unleash them. Your healthy recovery will have a lot to do with feelings, too. There is a great sense of peace that comes with getting comfortable with your moods, even your most uncomfortable moods. But how do you get there?

The mindful self is curious and open. It doesn't reject feelings, push them away, or stamp them as "bad." It is a gracious host. So just as you would get comfortable with a new friend, by spending time and asking questions, do the very same with your moods. Take an interest in your mood. Give it some attention. That doesn't mean analyzing the heck out of your mood, obsessing about it, or feeding into it. Adopt a quiet, calm, reflective stance. Look and listen. Breathe with it. Be gentle and compassionate.

Getting comfortable with moods means letting go of expectations. It means developing a deep, gracious acceptance of your own emotional state, whatever shape it happens to be in. Understand that everybody has these kinds of feelings and that all feelings—the so-called good, the bad, and the ugly—serve a purpose. We'll be talking more about the purpose of feelings in the next chapter, but for now, suffice it to say that your emotions aren't out to get you. Emotions are not your enemy. It may seem like feelings are causing you trouble, but the truth is that our *responses* to our feelings are what tend to cause problems. If you lash out at others when you experience anger, if you shut yourself away from loved ones when you feel sad, or if you quit doing things you care about when you get stressed, those actions will cause problems.

In our best possible lives, as our best possible selves, we learn to act in healthy ways *in spite of how we feel*. We notice, observe, and even embrace our moods without letting our feelings dictate our choices. We can be angry and nevertheless approach life from a place of calm. We can be sad and share it with others. We can feel stress and move through it gracefully and find our center. Not always. Okay, not even close to always. But a little bit more each day.

Next time you have a mood that you don't much enjoy, please greet it. Be polite and nonjudgmental. Breathe deeply. Send some light to that emotional space. Explore it. Be curious about it. Give yourself some grace. Understand that this mood will shift and flow and likely move on.

Getting comfortable with moods will take practice, and practice takes time. Be gentle with yourself in this process, and let yourself be the perfectly imperfect human you are!

Exercise: Practicing Liquid-Mood Meditation

As your mood arises, choose to engage with it from a place of curiosity. Breathe deeply and choose to sit with your feelings. Gift yourself with ten minutes of undistracted time. You are going to closely observe your mood.

With eyes closed, imagine your feelings as the liquid within the stone in a mood ring or a lava lamp. Watch the color develop. Watch it ebb and flow. Now imagine that liquid moving through your body. Take your time and notice its movements. Where does it collect? Where does it linger? Does it move freely or get stuck anywhere?

Next imagine the liquid is in a container with a little spout. Open the spout and let the liquid flow out of your body, slowly, gently, easily. See it moving freely from your body and collecting in a pool outside your body. Now the liquid is even clearer to you. Now you can dip your fingers into the liquid and explore it. Is it warm, hot, cold? Is it smooth or grainy? Is it what you expected? Have its colors changed in the fresh air? Do the colors seem to change as you look at them?

Play with this liquid for as long as you like. When you are finished, watch it evaporate. The liquid fades easily into the air and disappears. Take a deep cleansing breath, and thank your mood for arising, for moving as it needed to move, and for leaving.

Affirmations for Getting Comfortable with Moods

We recommend you say these affirmations out loud throughout the day to connect with your intention of a mindful recovery. We also recommend you type one affirmation into your smartphone each morning as a reminder to use it three to five times daily. You can download a printable copy of these affirmations at the website for this book: http://www.newharbinger.com/40705.

Monday: *Emotions are not my enemy.*

Tuesday: *Today I will not reject my emotions. I will get to know my emotions.*

Wednesday: *I can and will embrace my many moods in recovery.*

Thursday: *I can accept all my feelings today.*

Friday: *I choose my actions thoughtfully, despite how I feel.*

Saturday: *I greet my mood and explore it with curiosity.*

Sunday: *I accept my emotional state, whatever it may be.*

7

Gratitude for Feelings

So, there are two ways you can live: you can devote your life to staying in your comfort zone, or you can work on your freedom.

—**Michael A. Singer**

You have probably learned already that having an attitude of gratitude in recovery is simply a better way to live. When you are grateful, you open up to whatever life brings you. Pausing to be thankful for your experiences connects you to the present moment. The result is an amazing state of calm, pleasure, and contentment.

It is time to have an attitude of gratitude for your uncomfortable feelings. After years of resisting or running from these feelings, this may be hard to do. It's also hard to feel grateful for something when you can't see its purpose. So we will start there.

Imagine you found yourself in the middle of a foreign city. You couldn't speak the language, couldn't read the street signs, and didn't know which way to go. Along comes a tour guide, interpreting the language and steering you away from bad neighborhoods. You would feel pretty grateful, right? Well, your feelings are like that tour guide. They are giving you information, telling you what you need to know. While your feelings don't know everything (they need to be in balance with their partner, your mind), if you are willing to listen to them, your feelings have so much to teach you.

Fear gets a pretty bad rap, but it is actually a gift. And no question, when left to run wild, it can absolutely run amok. But fear is truly designed to keep you safe. People who try to live fearlessly act impulsively and end up getting hurt. You *should* be afraid to go skipping along the edge of a cliff. You *should* be afraid to steal from a store, yell at your boss, or drink milk ten days past its expiration date. Fear shows up to tell you about the consequences. There is certainly a healthy fear of relapse. It can keep your sneaky addictive thoughts from tricking you back into using. Fear can guide you back to the recovery behaviors that keep you strong. No, we don't want the fear of relapse to become overwhelming or to undermine your happy life in recovery. That wouldn't be productive. But some fear, realistic fear, protects you from the dangerous overconfidence that can sabotage you.

Anger, so misunderstood, is another gift. As Dr. Harriet Lerner (2014) pointed out in her classic book, *The Dance of Anger,* our anger tells us a lot about ourselves. It is a wise teacher, if we are willing to listen and learn. We tend to get angry when our boundaries are crossed, which means getting angry can help us find out where our boundaries actually are. As with all your emotions, spewing anger everywhere is not going to be helpful. But taking a mindful approach will help a lot. Notice your anger and use it wisely. Let it teach you what's important to you and what kind of treatment you expect from those around you.

Guilt can weigh heavily, especially in early recovery, but it too is a gift. It is telling you that you have a conscience. It is telling you the difference between right and wrong. If you stumble and act outside of your values, guilt comes along with a nudge. It reminds you to take ownership of your mistakes, so you can fix things and apologize if necessary. It helps you make better decisions. Listen to your guilt, and use it to guide how you live. (But if guilt has morphed into shame, telling you that you are somehow broken, defective, or worthless, don't listen! Talk to someone you trust and let them help you find your way out of there.)

Loneliness, usually hiding in a corner, is a gift, too. If you are willing to hear what it is whispering, you may find that you are being asked to find connection. Maybe it is time to try meetings, to call that acquaintance who could become a friend, or to let a loved one know what is really going on for you. Loneliness may be urging you to change your relationships. Or perhaps your loneliness is asking you to connect with yourself. Maybe it is time to sit quietly with your journal, breathe deeply, and see what happens. Imagine how you can use this time alone to further your goals in recovery.

Finally, even *sadness* is a gift and a guide. If you are willing to embrace it, you will see that sadness is telling you what matters most. It is singing to you about what you want, what you love. Sadness will teach you that loss is a part of life and that you are capable of living fully. You can tolerate your hurt. Sadness lets you know your heart is beating. It lets you know you were willing to take a risk. You may feel vulnerable and exposed in your hurt, but you are incredibly strong for feeling it. If you breathe into it and let it speak to you, there is so much to learn.

Your feelings are gifts. They are your guides. Don't neglect their wisdom by pushing them away. Welcome them!

Exercise: Finding Gratitude for Feelings

Gift yourself with twenty to thirty minutes of quiet time with your journal. Make a list of your most uncomfortable feelings, such as anger, frustration, fear, worry, stress, embarrassment, guilt, hurt, sadness, or loneliness. Provide at least one reason to be grateful for each feeling. Think about what the feeling is trying to teach you. If you can, give specific examples of what these feelings have offered you. Be patient with yourself as you make this powerful change in perspective.

Affirmations for Gratitude for Feelings

We recommend you say these affirmations out loud throughout the day to connect with your intention of a mindful recovery. We also recommend you type one affirmation into your smartphone each morning as a reminder to use it three to five times daily. You can download a printable copy of these affirmations at the website for this book: http://www.newharbinger.com/40705.

Monday: *I am open to my feelings and receive them as gifts.*

Tuesday: *Anger, fear, loneliness, guilt, and sadness are here to give me knowledge and strength.*

Wednesday: *My feelings are a guide to me today.*

Thursday: *I believe my emotions have something to teach me.*

Friday: *Even when I am uncomfortable, I know my feelings have a purpose.*

Saturday: *I am willing to learn from my feelings.*

Sunday: *I embrace my feelings and all of their wisdom.*

8

Soothing Anger

Let go or be dragged.

—**Zen proverb**

You probably aren't that scared of being poisoned. That's good, because other than your run-of-the-mill food poisoning, it's not really something you should be worrying about. But centuries ago in certain circles, mainly royal circles, it wasn't all that uncommon to get poisoned. And the reality was nothing like Romeo on stage, poetic and calm. It was gruesome. Blood might pour out of the mouth or come through the skin. The body might convulse or seize. The pain was excruciating, like the insides were being eaten away. Eventually poison will kill you, of course, but imagine the torture of those moments of living with it inside your body!

There is a point to this horror story, we promise. You see, it has been said that walking around angry is a lot like drinking poison and hoping the *other* person dies.

When you are carrying anger in your body and mind, what happens? What does it do to your mood, your relationships, your day? When you are angry, who really suffers?

Walking around with the poison of anger eating away at your insides is not going to help your recovery. It won't allow you to find peace. Chances are high that you will relapse. Chances are even higher that, relapsed or not, you will be miserable.

Anger, like all your feelings, is natural and even healthy. We aren't suggesting that you ignore, reject, hide from, or be ashamed of your anger. But it is time to take an honest look at whether your anger is helping or hurting you. Is it productive? Are you using it as a guidepost, telling you what you want and need so that you can make positive changes? Or is it dominating you, making every moment harder than it needs to be?

There's a saying in recovery: "If you meet three jerks in a day, look at yourself because you are the jerk." This might be tough to acknowledge, but if everyone or everything is making you angry, it is probably not a case of bad luck. Odds are it's about you. It has something to do with your mood or your way of thinking. Maybe you have slipped into self-pity or a bit of narcissism. You are angry because the world isn't behaving as you think it should. People aren't behaving the way you would. Things aren't happening as you planned, and you aren't in control. Or maybe you just woke up on the wrong side of the bed. The fix isn't going to happen in the world around you; it is going to be found *within you.*

As with all your experiences, acknowledge your anger. Greet it with gentle compassion. Approach it with curiosity. Acknowledge, too, that there is probably another feeling underneath the anger. We therapists call anger a *secondary emotion.* A different feeling, usually one that makes you feel vulnerable, comes first. Face it: being angry seems a lot safer than feeling some other emotions. There is a sense of having your guard up, having your armor on. If you peel back your anger, what do you find hiding there? Hurt, sadness, worry, shame? Name the feeling if you can. Even if you can't find the underlying feeling, consider that they might be there. Then offer that part of yourself some kindness and support.

If you are being poisoned by your anger, know it. Breathe deeply and decide to make your life better. Decide to let it go. Bring yourself back to this decision that you have made to recover. You have chosen to live life mindfully and to pursue serenity and happiness. Anything that is getting in the way of this new life isn't serving you well. It is worth letting go of. Be willing to try some of the following techniques for releasing your anger and finding peace.

Exercise 1: Cooling Your Anger

Many people describe anger as carrying some heat with it, maybe even burning like fire. Some people describe their rage by saying they "see red." One way to soothe your anger is to *cool* it. If you find yourself feeling angry, wash your hands in cool water, especially letting the water fall over your wrists. Take a cool, refreshing shower. Close your eyes and visualize the hot red areas of your body being bathed in cool blue light. Drink a big glass of ice water. Chew or suck on crushed ice. Buy some smooth stones, the kind sold at plant nurseries or art supply stores, and keep them in the fridge so that when you feel angry you can place a stone on your forehead, heart, or palm. Notice what happens to the heat of anger when you practice the art of cooling yourself down.

Exercise 2: Practicing Grace

If you are comfortable praying, try this prayer. Every day for two weeks, pray for the person you are angry with to receive everything that you would want for yourself. This is just an exercise. You don't have to really mean it. However, if you find yourself just saying the words without meaning them, acknowledge that experience. Allow yourself to be exactly where you are right now. It may change over time, or it may not. Give yourself some grace, and see how it feels to pray for this person. What happens to your anger?

Affirmations for Soothing Anger

We recommend you say these affirmations out loud throughout the day to connect with your intention of a mindful recovery. We also recommend you type one affirmation into your smartphone each morning as a reminder to use it three to five times daily. You can download a printable copy of these affirmations at the website for this book: http://www.newharbinger.com/40705.

Monday: *I am not owned by anger. I choose to cultivate peace.*

Tuesday: *I soothe myself with cooling blue light.*

Wednesday: *It is okay to feel angry. I approach my anger with gentleness and compassion.*

Thursday: *I have many ways to cope with anger. I can use as many methods as I want or need to help me when I am angry.*

Friday: *I will not let my anger at others poison me. I choose to release my anger and live my life happily.*

Saturday: *Like all my feelings, anger is temporary.*

Sunday: *I know how to put out this fire. I choose to cool my anger.*

9

Releasing Fear

If you have not lived through something, it is not true.

—Kabir

By the rules of comic books, if you want to create a monster, start with a pretty basic creature and then expose it to toxic waste. Take a baby alligator, for example, and blast it with some radiation. It will become a beast of unholy proportions, leave a trail of mass destruction, and be stopped only by an army and a team of scientists. Finding yourself with a baby alligator may not have been easy to begin with, but now we're talking about the darn thing crushing skyscrapers and taking out bridges.

Similarly, to create a state of utter chaos, you take a regular problem and radiate it with fear. The problem will become gargantuan. Worse yet, you won't be able see a solution. You will feel so overwhelmed, you probably won't believe that there *is* a solution. Your wisdom will be out of reach. You can't hear that calm, clear voice inside of you when fear is roaring away.

Fear won't let anyone else help you either. It keeps you isolated. A fearful dog will literally bite the hand that feeds it. An effort to connect or an offer of support can be seen as an attack when you are in fear. There is a saying in recovery: "The phone weighs a thousand pounds." Picking up the phone to reach out to others can feel damn near impossible. Fear is that weight.

In chapter 7, we talked about the benefits of fear. Fear serves a purpose, just like all our feelings do. Unfortunately, the natural healthy fear that can guide and inspire us is often overrun by the misplaced, misdirected, and frenzied fear that tends to dominate us. That frenzied fear can easily fall into one of two categories: the fear of losing what you have or the fear of not getting what you want. The solution to each is the same.

"When I got into treatment," Lydia says, "I learned that I had a choice when it came to fear: I could Forget Everything And Run, or I could Face Everything And Recover."

The only real way to face everything and recover is to develop faith; this could be faith in God, a higher power, nature, or the natural flow of life that is always there to support you. It could be faith in yourself, trusting that you have the ability to cope with what comes your way. It could be faith in your loved ones, knowing that they will be there for you when you need them. If you can truly develop your faith in whatever ways work best for you, fear will fall away.

Acknowledge your fear and the problems it causes you. See how fear has driven your addiction. When fear arises, let it rise and look it in the face. Breathe in. Breathe out. In that single moment of stillness, find your faith.

Exercise: Rewriting Your Ghost Stories

Most of us are carrying around a lot of fears. But luckily, a lot of these fears are based on scary stories, not on reality. Most of us don't believe in ghosts anymore, but our lives are full of ghost stories, nonetheless. For this exercise, you will be bringing your wisdom and your faith along and doing a rewrite. It is time to let go of the ghost stories that are keeping you afraid.

Find a favorite pen and a quiet place to sit with your journal. Breathe deeply, close your eyes, and gently ask for your fears to become clear to you. When a fear becomes clear, open your eyes and write it down.

Now ask yourself this question: Why? What is really scary about this? Why am I afraid? When an answer arises, write that down. Now ask the questions again. Continue this process until you feel you have come to the end of your scary story.

For example, maybe you are afraid of being late to work. Why? *Because my boss might get mad at me.* Why is that scary? *Because I am afraid of losing my job.* What is so scary about that? *I am afraid I will never get another job.* Why is that scary? *I will not have any money.* And what's so scary about that? *I'm afraid I will end up living on the streets.* Now that is a very scary story.

Once you have finished writing your ghost story and can take an honest look at it, it is time to release your fear. Find places to insert faith. Look for places to insert faith in yourself, faith in a higher power, or faith in others. This is how you will rewrite the story. Using the example above, maybe you can find faith in your company, reminding yourself that they don't fire people over little things. Maybe you can find faith in yourself, telling yourself that you would be able to find another job if you did get fired. Maybe you can find faith in your loved ones, understanding that they would help out so you wouldn't end up on the streets.

Practice this exercise whenever you find yourself caught up in fear. You don't need to be haunted by ghost stories in recovery!

Affirmations for Releasing Fear

We recommend you say these affirmations out loud throughout the day to connect with your intention of a mindful recovery. We also recommend you type one affirmation into your smartphone each morning as a reminder to use it three to five times daily. You can download a printable copy of these affirmations at the website for this book: http://www .newharbinger.com/40705.

Monday:	*When I encounter fear, I choose to face everything and recover.*
Tuesday:	*Today I will ask myself what I really need. I have the capacity to nurture myself.*
Wednesday:	*I am not my fear.*
Thursday:	*I trust the universe to provide what I need.*
Friday:	*I can see my problems clearly, at their true and manageable size.*
Saturday:	*I understand and believe that I can tolerate loss.*
Sunday:	*I move through fear. Fear does not control me.*

10

Accepting Everyday Frustration

Just let go. Let go of how you thought your life should be, and embrace the life that is trying to work its way into your consciousness.

—**Caroline Myss**

You've probably heard it before: Don't sweat the small stuff.

Traffic. Crowds. Lines. They got your order wrong at the drive-through. Your cell phone is malfunctioning. The meeting usually makes you feel better, but today everyone just complained.

This is the so-called small stuff. When you have a lot of ideas about how things and people are supposed to be, little things that get in the way can seem like a disaster. Not sweating the small stuff is really about keeping your perspective: realize what is small and what is big, and don't confuse the two.

Here is one easy way to remember to change your perspective when the small stuff is looming large. Tell yourself to ROLL with it: to *realize obstacles are life lessons*. See every apparent obstacle as an opportunity. The truth is if you always got what you wanted, if life always ran smoothly, things would get pretty dull. You wouldn't learn much, and you wouldn't grow. What you see as complications or stressors may really be gifts.

Changing the way you talk, even to yourself, also comes in handy when you want a change in perspective. If you are used to saying things like *I can't stand traffic*, it is time to try something new, like *I don't enjoy traffic, but it's no big deal. This isn't my favorite thing, but I can handle it. I don't need things to go smoothly all the time. I'm not the only one stuck in traffic, and I won't be the only one running behind today.*

You might also try shifting your mind-set from *taking* to *giving*. That's a dramatic shift. Most of us walk around thinking about ourselves pretty much all day long. Instead of thinking about how your needs aren't getting met in a small-stuff moment, think about what you can offer. See where you can improve the situation. If the meeting is full of negativity, say something positive. If the checkout girl is grumpy and rude, be warm and kind. If you feel like no one cares about you, give someone a call and show you care about *them*.

Finally, address your stress. Ignoring the so-called small stuff is just as unproductive as making it seem bigger than it is. You don't have to sweat it, but you do have to deal with it. Instead of ignoring your stress, understand it. Acknowledge to yourself, *I wasn't expecting such a big crowd here today; I feel kind of overwhelmed.* Notice where that feeling is lingering in your body. Breathe into that space and release your stress as you exhale. Offer yourself some compassion: *Nobody likes to feel overwhelmed. It's okay. I can deal with it.* Don't be afraid to soothe yourself the way you would a child or a friend. Pat or stroke your own hand or shoulder, play with your hair, roll your shoulders around in a circle, or sway gently in your chair. Feel the tension lessen.

At the end of the day, how you move through the world is up to you. Life is always in session, and small stuff comes up. You could be a pinball, bouncing forcefully from moment to moment in your life. You could let any obstacle change your direction, letting frustrations fling you from place to place. If you've been living life as a pinball, it can be hard to see the alternative. The world you've been inhabiting, that crazy pinball machine, is loud and full of flashing lights. There is chaos. There is drama. There is a great deal of motion. In addiction, there can be something almost, well, addictive, about the insanity that results from being bounced around. There is excitement there. A lot of people see recovery as the end of all pleasure and joy, as if releasing your addiction were the death of fun.

But if you picked up this book, you must have some desire and some willingness to become peaceful. Or at the very least, you want to be present for your life. (That's hard to do when you are being flung from one frustration to the next.) Mindfulness is not about flash or chaos. It is found in moments of stillness and calm, where most things of importance will be found.

If you are no longer a pinball, what will you be? Well, that is up to you. Maybe you will be a breeze moving through the branches of a tree. You encounter the leaves and the branches but flow around them, continuing on to where you want to be. Maybe you will be water in a stream, flowing gracefully over and around the stones in your path. Maybe you will continue to be your recovering self, perfectly imperfect in a perfectly imperfect world, and learning to flow through the frustrations of everyday life.

Exercise: Accepting Everyday Frustration

For the next week, notice your everyday frustrations. Ask yourself in a frustrated moment whether you want to be a pinball. Realize the wasted time and energy that happens when you let the small stuff catapult you from place to place. Breathe deeply in that moment. Remember to ROLL with it: realize obstacles are life lessons. Make a new choice. Imagine yourself as water flowing or as a soft cool breeze. Give yourself a moment to truly imagine yourself flowing *with* your life, not fighting against it. Notice how this feels.

Affirmations for Accepting Everyday Frustration

We recommend you say these affirmations out loud throughout the day to connect with your intention of a mindful recovery. We also recommend you type one affirmation into your smartphone each morning as a reminder to use it three to five times daily. You can download a printable copy of these affirmations at the website for this book: http://www.newharbinger.com/40705.

Monday: *Today I flow through my obstacles smoothly.*

Tuesday: *Today I realize obstacles are life lessons, and I can ROLL with them.*

Wednesday: *Things seldom go as I expect, and that is okay with me.*

Thursday: *I can see that the small stuff is the stuff of life, and it is manageable.*

Friday: *I notice the small stuff and don't let it build up. Today I address my stress.*

Saturday: *Just as my breath flows in and out, I flow from moment to moment.*

Sunday: *If the small stuff seems big, I can change my perspective. I can bring it back to its actual size.*

SECTION 3

Especially Strong Emotions

11
What to Do with Especially Strong Feelings

And you? When will you begin that long journey into yourself?

—**Rumi**

It will come as no surprise to you that intense emotions are part of your recovery journey. Sometimes it may feel like your emotions come from out of the clear blue sky. Using substances and engaging in destructive behaviors were specifically designed to help you avoid, sidestep, and otherwise ignore feelings of loneliness, rage, despair, jealousy, and crushing anxiety. Well, putting your head in the sand when it comes to strong feelings simply doesn't work. In fact, disregarding these feelings will actually make them hang around longer. As the Swiss psychoanalyst Carl Jung has said, "What you resist persists." Trying to hide from strong feelings or to push them away is a strategy that is doomed to fail.

Again, your emotions serve an important purpose. Even your strong feelings are worthwhile. They remind you that you are a person who really cares. Chances are you care a lot.

You can also use your strong feelings as a guide to help you figure out what is really going on for you. The more you know what is really going on, the better chance you will have to embrace a healthy recovery. Are you ready to take a closer look? More importantly, are you ready to reap the rewards of knowing yourself better?

Most people ask, "What do I do with my intense feelings? How do I get rid of them?" Well, the short and strange answer is to do nothing. Along this recovery journey, there will be times when doing nothing is the right thing to do. Here we are asking you to notice what the feeling is and to just wait. Don't react. Don't do anything.

At other times, there will be opportunities to act. But in order to act wisely, you must have the skills to calm your mind down and act from a place of *values*, which is just a fancy way of saying "This is the type of person I want to be." You will have a deepening sense of your own values as you get to know yourself in recovery, and this book will help you explore and define them. But even when your values are well defined, strong feelings can cause you to act against them. That's why starting with a calm, nonreactive stance is so important. When encountering strong feelings, pause. Consider the following ideas.

First, in Buddhism, the central idea is that life is suffering (*suffering* here means imbalance). If you can understand this concept and not fight with it, then the natural next step is to realize that things are not going to be perfect for you. Okay, we said it. Things are not going to be perfect for you. You may already know that, but if you are like most of us, you have not quite *accepted* it yet. You are still trying to avoid suffering. As you pause and notice these strong feelings of yours, understand that they are natural. They are a normal and natural part of the human experience. You don't need to go to war with these feelings. Breathe deeply and know this: *Where you are at this moment is exactly where you are supposed to be.*

Second, accept that you are not in control. This is similar to the first step in Alcoholics Anonymous. It goes right back to the idea that if you let things be as they are (without a knockdown, drag-out fight), the intense feelings will dissolve. Or at least the intensity of your feelings will decrease. Accept that occasionally you will have intense feelings. That's okay, and you are okay too. Awareness and acceptance of your strong feelings will transform them into something smaller and lighter.

Third, take just one of your intense feelings, let's say loneliness, and see if anything there needs your attention. Invite loneliness in, offer it a cup of coffee, let it sit in your favorite comfy chair, and sit across from loneliness and ask it this one question: *What do you need now?* Give your feeling a chance to answer this question. If loneliness is the unbearable feeling you are experiencing, what you may need now is to experience the feeling without judgment. What you will notice is that you can survive this feeling. What would it be like to show kindness to your feeling? Notice if the intensity of the feeling is diminishing. Is the level of intensity going from a 10 (very intense) to a 5 (moderately intense), or even to a 3 (mildly intense)? Great. You have just experienced how strong feelings work in recovery.

Audio for the next meditation exercise is available at http://www .newharbinger.com/40705.

Exercise: Respecting Especially Strong Feelings

Even strong feelings can be your guide in recovery. For this meditation, sit in a comfortable space and close your eyes. Give yourself ten minutes. Begin to breathe, inhaling through your nose and exhaling through your mouth. Slow your breathing down. Notice the breath come in through both of your nostrils and leave through your slightly open mouth. Allow whatever intense feeling you have into the room with you. Now name your feeling—*hatred, fury, spite, isolation, desperation, terror, exhaustion,* or some other intense feeling. Give your strong feeling the same respect you would give a beloved teacher or a respected coach. Now quietly greet the feeling by saying *Hello _____. I'm so glad you showed up today. What would you like to teach me today? I am open to whatever you have in mind.*

Reflect on what comes up. Now, invite *patience* into the room with you. Introduce patience to your intense feeling. For example, *Loneliness, this is patience. Patience, this is loneliness.* Let them get to know each other. Remember, they are both within you. You have the opportunity to let them hang out together or meet up again at any time.

Affirmations for Especially Strong Feelings

We recommend you say these affirmations out loud throughout the day to connect with your intention of a mindful recovery. We also recommend you type one affirmation into your smartphone each morning as a reminder to use it three to five times daily. You can download a printable copy of these affirmations at the website for this book: http://www .newharbinger.com/40705.

Monday:	*Today I allow all my feelings to exist without judgment.*
Tuesday:	*Thank you, feelings, for showing up as my guide today.*
Wednesday:	*What is the next thing I need today?*
Thursday:	*Today I remind myself to slow down and rebalance.*
Friday:	*Breathing is a natural way to dissolve intense feelings.*
Saturday:	*The gift of not attaching to my feelings is heartfelt.*
Sunday:	*Even my strongest feelings in recovery are not permanent.*

12

When Emotions Get Stuck

You need no one's permission but your own to be whole.

—Michael Bernard Beckwith

Marcus quit drinking four months ago, but he was not feeling any better. In fact, he felt worse. He had lots of sleepless nights, and when he did sleep, his nightmares woke him up in a cold sweat. Most days, he couldn't get the images out of his mind of his best friend getting shot. He would go to the grocery store at one o'clock in the morning, when no one was in the store except one or two clerks. He avoided people at all costs. Marcus wasn't even able to go to his daughter's school play, because he could not bring himself to pass the corner where his friend died. He wore headphones at his construction job, so he would not have to interact with anyone. And most people, including his wife, just left him alone. He felt like he was stuck in quicksand, unable to move.

Marcus has a condition called post-traumatic stress disorder (PTSD). This condition can leave you feeling tense and out of control. PTSD is the result of experiencing or witnessing an extremely disturbing event, like military combat, a violent assault, a natural disaster, a sexual assault, or childhood abuse. Some people go through a traumatic experience and do not have difficulties, while others struggle daily with unwanted thoughts and distressing feelings about the event. Unwanted thoughts could include unending negative self-talk. Distressing feelings could include uncontrolled anxiety, intense anger, and penetrating depression. Some people even experience related physical or medical problems, like an increase in headaches or a surge in overall body pain. Clearly, experiencing a traumatic event can have short- and long-term consequences for your recovery. You may have some of the same feelings Marcus has, or you may just feel stuck in a bad mood without knowing why you are feeling so out of balance.

If you have used drugs or alcohol to attempt to escape these distressing thoughts and feelings, you are not alone. According to research, 52 percent of men and 28 percent of women who have PTSD also have an alcohol problem that turns into addiction. The numbers for drug abuse are similar: 35 percent of men and 27 percent of women who have PTSD also have a drug problem that turns into addiction (McCauley et al. 2012).

You may not know that your brain is trying to help you cope. When you experience a traumatic event, like Marcus did, your brain produces endorphins. Endorphins are chemical messengers that decrease pain and increase a feeling of pleasure. Your brain releases these feel-good endorphins to help you cope with the stress you are feeling. That's an incredible thing for your brain to do.

However, when the stressful event is over, the body experiences withdrawal from the endorphins. Believe it or not, endorphin withdrawal has some of the same symptoms as withdrawal from drugs or alcohol. If you experience endorphin withdrawal, you will feel super anxious, sad, and even may feel physical pain. You will experience an increase in cravings for alcohol or drugs.

So, you see, even though your brain is trying very hard to help you feel better, it may also be working to lead you back to using drugs and alcohol. And this means that you need to increase your coping skills when it comes to recovery from stuck emotions. This usually requires getting additional support from a trained therapist and/or a recovery group for folks who have both trauma and addiction. Experiencing a traumatic event does not mean you must remain stuck reliving the event over and over again. It does mean that if you are aware of the event's impact on you, you have a great chance to change how you think and feel about yourself.

Audio for the next meditation exercise is available at http://www .newharbinger.com/40705.

Exercise: Practicing Loving-Kindness Meditation

If you are reliving a distressing event from your past, it is important to remind yourself that the event is exactly that: an event in your life. The event does not define who you are as a person. Next, thank your brain for producing endorphins to help you get through the rough time in your life. Then find a quiet place with few interruptions. Sit comfortably. Take three beautiful deep breaths to release any tension you may be feeling. Use this Buddhist loving-kindness meditation (Salzburg 2002), which is intended to soothe your body and mind and bring you peace. Are you ready? Say aloud:

May I be free from fear and anger.

May I be free from danger.

May I be peaceful and happy.

May I be at ease in my own body and mind.

May my love for myself flow boundlessly.

You can repeat this loving-kindness meditation as many times as you would like. We suggest saying it out loud at least three times, although at the beginning, you may want to repeat it many more times.

After you have said it, close your eyes. Take three more nice deep breaths. What do you notice? Be aware of yourself in the present moment. You are on your way to being unstuck.

Affirmations for When Emotions Get Stuck

We recommend you say these affirmations out loud throughout the day to connect with your intention of a mindful recovery. We also recommend you type one affirmation into your smartphone each morning as a reminder to use it three to five times daily. You can download a printable copy of these affirmations at the website for this book: http://www .newharbinger.com/40705.

Monday:	*My distressing experiences do not define who I am as a person.*
Tuesday:	*My recovery embraces healing from past experiences.*
Wednesday:	*Today I reflect on my strengths and what is important to me.*
Thursday:	*Being mindful of healing is my intention today.*
Friday:	*I am building my ability to soothe myself today.*
Saturday:	*Today I will connect with loved ones.*
Sunday:	*I focus my attention on being mentally, physically, and spiritually well.*

13

Honoring and Releasing
Old Ways of Coping

*The only way to make sense out of change is to plunge
into it, move with it, and join the dance.*

—Alan Watts

Carol just got the news in a text. Lucas broke up with her after five months of dating. She was heartbroken; she really liked Lucas and thought they were going to be in a long-term relationship. They had so much fun together, or so she thought. Carol had stopped drinking and smoking pot almost a year ago, but she still found herself reverting to old ways to numb her feelings, especially those vulnerable sad feelings. After she got the breakup text, she went online and started to shop for clothes, shoes, handbags, and even pet clothes for her new puppy. Then, before she hit the purchase button, a lightbulb went off in her head. "My old ways of dealing with my feelings won't work this time," she said out loud.

The instant rush of buying things would no doubt be followed by even more sadness and loneliness. Not to mention more debt on her credit card. Carol decided not to press "purchase" this time. Instead, she acknowledged her old ways of managing sadness. She remembered she smoked pot and drank heavily after a breakup two years ago. She also remembered that avoiding the discomfort of her loss did not help, because she usually ended up feeling more withdrawn and alone. Was it possible that the usual way of coping caused the problem to linger longer than it needed to? She decided, right then and there, to let go of her old unhealthy way of coping with loss and replace it with a healthier way of coping.

Old ways of coping, like using drugs and alcohol or engaging in risky behaviors, may have given you an instant disconnection from painful feelings. But somehow the intense feelings came rushing back in. And now that you are in recovery, you may still be using behaviors to disengage from what is really going on, or you may be avoiding unpleasant feelings altogether. Sometimes you may wait until the very last minute to admit that something is upsetting you. Then you explode. Or you may not communicate at all. Stuffing how you feel is an old way of coping.

Drinking or using drugs or some other risky behavior was a way of coping that temporarily worked in the past. It let you check out or not care about the problem. You must respect and honor that you were trying to protect your emotional life. Then there came a time when it didn't work anymore. In your recovery, you have released your old ways of coping with life's stressors. But there is a void, and now you are going to fill that void. We are introducing you to new ways of coping that will be your go-to methods when you are going through a tough time. We want you to have *options*. Keep in mind that there is no cure to fix all the challenges in life. But there are different and healthy options to lean on when things get rough.

Exercise: Identifying New Ways of Coping

Mindfulness rewires your brain to be able to tolerate discomfort and reduce cravings. According to research (Hölzel et al. 2011), using mindfulness has been shown to increase your ability to manage your emotions. Notice your thoughts and feelings without reacting to them. Be curious and kind to yourself. After all, your mind is just doing its job.

This mindfulness exercise has two parts. The first part is to honor and allow yourself to let go of the past ways you've handled difficult experiences that didn't quite work. Start by focusing on a recent event. Identify what got you hot and bothered. For Carol, it was the breakup text from Lucas, and the feeling was sadness. What is your event and what is the feeling tied to that event?

Okay, whatever your feelings are, remember that your mind is doing its best to take care of you. Now we will add mindfulness to your coping toolbox.

The second part of this exercise is to bring in new energy with four new coping strategies to handle any current challenge. Most likely you are already familiar with these coping strategies, and that's good. This is your opportunity to add these strategies back into your recovery. We call these coping skills JOLT, because they are intended to jolt you out of old ways of reacting and offer an alternative way to respond to stressors:

J: Journal. To help you slow down and reconnect with yourself and your emotional life, write down what is happening in the here and now.

O: Observe your breath. Focus on your inhale and your exhale and begin to slow your breathing down a bit. Release the negative thoughts on the out-breath, and breathe in positive messages on the in-breath.

L: Listen to music. Choose a song or album that inspires you and gives you a change of mood and energy. Depending on what will be most helpful in the circumstances, this could be calm music or something more upbeat.

T: Take a walk. Never underestimate the benefit of getting up and getting outside for a brief stroll. It could be a ten-minute walk around the block of your office building or neighborhood, or it could be a longer walk.

You can decide how to best use these JOLT strategies. Maybe you will use one each day, or you will grab a strategy when you are feeling stressed. JOLT increases your ability to be flexible and adapt how you react to stressors that will occur in your recovery.

Affirmations for Honoring and Releasing Old Ways of Coping

We recommend you say these affirmations out loud throughout the day to connect with your intention of a mindful recovery. We also recommend you type one affirmation into your smartphone each morning as a reminder to use it three to five times daily. You can download a printable copy of these affirmations at the website for this book: http://www .newharbinger.com/40705.

Monday: *I make room for new ways of coping with challenges.*

Tuesday: *Today is dedicated to one creative way to manage stress.*

Wednesday: *Releasing old ways of coping benefits my recovery.*

Thursday: *I can tolerate discomfort today.*

Friday: *My new ways of coping with stress are improving my mood.*

Saturday: *My mind is flexible when it comes to finding solutions to problems.*

Sunday: *Today I observe any stress with curiosity and kindness.*

14

Letting Pain Be Pain, Not Suffering

Wherever you are is the perfect place to awaken. This moment is the exact place to practice compassion and loving awareness. You have all the ingredients to breathe and find freedom just where you are.

—Jack Kornfield

What is the true difference between pain and suffering? Pain is a distressing sensation. It could be physical (including chronic pain), or it could be emotional distress. Pain is unavoidable: a migraine headache, a sore back, a broken heart. These things are *really* painful. Most of us have experienced these or other intense pain sensations. You might have used substances to help decrease your pain. You might even be in some type of pain right now as you read this.

So how is pain any different from suffering? Ask yourself these questions. Is your identity tied up in your pain? Do you find yourself talking about your pain to anyone who will listen? Is your pain the first thing you think of when you wake up in the morning and the last thought you have at the end of the day? Do you organize your daytime hours around managing your pain? If your pain is taking over a large part of each day, you may be moving into *suffering*. The biggest difference between pain and suffering is that pain is unavoidable, but suffering is optional.

Suffering is the result of resisting your pain. It happens when you focus on your pain, refuse to accept that it exists, and throw extra feelings on top of it, like anger or anxiety or shame. If you find yourself focusing all your attention on your pain, it's time to try a new way of thinking. First, we are going to ask you to acknowledge your relationship with pain. Then we are going to ask you to change the story you are telling yourself about your pain. You may notice your old pain story. Perhaps your old pain story sounds like this:

My pain is getting worse.

No one understands how hurt I feel.

Why can't my body cooperate?

I would be much happier if it weren't for this upsetting situation.

I can't get through a week without excruciating pain.

These old stories, as comfortable and familiar as they are, lead to suffering. Suffering loves your company. Suffering loves nothing better than to hang out with you, sleep over, greet you in the morning, and meet your friends and family. This old story deserves a fresh rewrite.

Your new story may feel odd and awkward at first. We are asking you to *let pain be pain*. Accept pain as it is, without the need to judge it or change it. Notice the pain. Observe the pain and offer it your curious attention. Here are some new pain stories you can entertain:

I am present with this experience.

I observe this sensation.

I look at this experience from five feet away.

I am curious about my body.

This feeling is temporary. I can ride it out.

Remember, you are creating a new and different relationship with pain, and breaking old habits is not always easy. This is a more accepting relationship, with more awareness and compassion and less struggle. Instead of fighting your pain, you are developing a mindful connection with it. We are asking something radical here. We are suggesting that you welcome the pain into your life. Be present with it. Notice what is happening within your body and mind, and do this without judgment.

As you change your relationship to your pain, the pain no longer moves into unending suffering. And your thoughts and feelings about the pain can pass without getting stuck. You are letting pain be and allowing your thoughts to move freely.

Exercise: Calming the Nervous System

To begin to change your relationship with pain, we will be guiding you through an ancient yoga technique called *palming*. This is a yoga exercise to calm the eyes and central nervous system. The eyes are very sensitive and need your attention. Looking at a computer, television, tablet, or cell phone for many hours each day has an impact on your eyes, your mind, and your nervous system.

For this palming exercise, it is recommended that you wash your hands with warm water before you start. Sit comfortably in a quiet place. If you are wearing glasses, take them off and place them near you. Spend a couple of minutes sitting with your back against the back of your chair. Notice your breathing. Next, open your eyes, keep your head and neck still, and relax your shoulders. As if there were a clock in front of you, move your eyes up to the twelve o'clock position and hold for a second. Then move your eyes to the six o'clock position and hold for a moment. Do this up-and-down eye exercise five times. Then bring your hands in front of you, rubbing your palms together until you feel warm heat. Close your eyes, and gently cup your palms over your closed eyes. Ahhh. Feel the healing heat around your eyes. Notice your breathing. Wonderful. Feel a sense of quiet. Let yourself settle down for a few moments.

Next, bring your palms down, open your eyes, imagining the clock again, and begin to move your eyes from left to right, from nine o'clock to three o'clock. Hold at nine o'clock for a moment and three o'clock for a moment. Practice this movement five times, and then go back to palming. Rub your palms together and generate heat. Gently place your palms over your closed eyes. Once again, breathe and let any tension or pain release from your eyes and your body. Breathe. Very nice.

Ready for the final exercise? Open your eyes one more time, and as you imagine the clock, move your eyes in a diagonal direction, two o'clock down to eight o'clock. Do this diagonal movement five times. Then, switch to the other diagonal, eleven o'clock down to five o'clock. After you have completed these diagonal movements five times, go back to your palming. Rub your palms together in front of you until you feel warmth. Gently place your warm palms over your closed eyes. Amazing. Breathe. You have just experienced the calming of your central nervous system. And a calm nervous system is the foundation of moving through pain.

Affirmations for Letting Pain Be Pain

We recommend you say these affirmations out loud throughout the day to connect with your intention of a mindful recovery. We also recommend you type one affirmation into your smartphone each morning as a reminder to use it three to five times daily. You can download a printable copy of these affirmations at the website for this book: http://www .newharbinger.com/40705.

Monday: *Today I notice pain and choose to let it move through me.*

Tuesday: *Pain is a natural experience in the body, not something to fight with.*

Wednesday: *I am aware of the sensation of pain, and I relax into the sensation.*

Thursday: *Suffering is optional, and I choose a new story.*

Friday: *I invite pain as an opportunity to learn something new about my body.*

Saturday: *I send love to my body today through my breath.*

Sunday: *I separate pain from suffering with kindness and compassion.*

The Gift of Recovery

15

Self-Compassion

*We cannot ignore our pain and have
compassion for it at the same time.*

—Brené Brown

Joanne started pacing back and forth in front of her best friend, Sam. "I
was this close," she said, and held up her trembling hand with her thumb
and finger a half an inch apart. "I almost used yesterday. What an idiot.
I almost threw away three years of sobriety. Have you ever heard of
someone so stupid?"

Sam sat back in his chair and took a breath. He was calm and patient.
"Listen, don't beat yourself up. Wasn't yesterday the anniversary of your
sister's accident?"

Joanne's eyes welled up. She sat down and took a deep breath. "Yeah,
I guess I pushed that out of my mind."

Sam understood. "You made it through, and you've come a long way
in three years. Having urges to use is normal, especially around anniversary dates. It's okay. You're human; we're all human."

Joanne looked at Sam, grateful and, for a moment, relieved. "Thank
you. That's why you're my best friend: you understand what I've been
through." Joanne felt better. Having Sam listen and give her encouraging
words was a lifesaver.

Do you ever feel that your close friends are kinder to you when you
have a problem than you are to yourself? Do you ever feel like you care

more about your spouse, your close friend, a family member, or even someone from work than you care about yourself? Perhaps what is missing here is this thing called *self-compassion*. Self-compassion is the experience of being as kind to yourself as a good friend would be to you. This is especially powerful in recovery from addictive behaviors.

Addiction brings its share of negative and punishing thoughts. If you are in the middle of a strong urge to use, in the past you either acted on that urge or did everything humanly possible to beat that urge into submission, including berating yourself for having the urge. Self-compassion offers you another choice.

Showing compassion for yourself is the ability to slow down, notice the agitation you are feeling in your mind and body, and offer yourself a small prayer of encouragement. It's the ability to give yourself the benefit of the doubt when things get tough. And things will get tough. Self-compassion can help you cope with the urges in a nonjudgmental way. It feels like a warm, friendly hand on your shoulder. Suddenly the tension leaves your body, and the oversensitive mind calms down.

You need a way to remind yourself to show kindness to the person who may need it the most: *you*. The goal here is to build up a self-compassion bank account. Start small with a few kind words or phrases to yourself, and add more as you move through life's ups and downs.

Exercise: Writing About Self-Compassion

This self-compassion meditation is a writing meditation. It's an opportunity to reflect on a challenging time you have been having in your recovery. You will need your journal or a notepad and a pen. Find a quiet place in your home or outside.

At the top of the page, write down what the problem or challenge is. Draw a line down the middle of the page. On the right side of the page, write down things you say to yourself that are not especially supportive. On the left side of the page, write down comments that your best friend would say to you. Here's an example.

Challenge: *I got really angry at my partner.*	
Best Friend's Supportive Words	**Unsupportive Self-Critique**
It's okay. You did the best you could with the information you had.	I should have known better.
Give yourself some time to figure out what happened.	Why did I get so angry at him? My anger is out of control.
You make good decisions. Give yourself a chance to see what unfolds.	Why did I choose to walk out? I don't like how I acted.
It's understandable that you feel alone sometimes. That's normal.	I shouldn't have texted him. I sound desperate.
You will get through this and make the choice that is healthy for you.	How am I going to talk to him again after how I treated him?

Great job. Now, fold the page right down the middle. Reread the supportive statements that your best friend would say to you. Okay. Now read them once more. This is the beginning of self-compassion. How does it feel to be your own best friend for a few minutes? The more you channel your inner best friend when you are having a difficult time, the more natural it will become. Congratulations! You are on your way to experiencing more self-compassion in your recovery.

Affirmations for Self-Compassion

We recommend you say these affirmations out loud throughout the day to connect with your intention of a mindful recovery. We also recommend you type one affirmation into your smartphone each morning as a reminder to use it three to five times daily. You can download a printable copy of these affirmations at the website for this book: http://www .newharbinger.com/40705.

Monday: *I care for myself the same way I would care for a close friend.*

Tuesday: *Today being kind to myself is my top priority.*

Wednesday: *I understand that there are challenges in my recovery, and I am able to face them.*

Thursday: *Today I will support my own ideas and goals with respect and support.*

Friday: *I meet each day of my recovery with gentleness.*

Saturday: *When I have a self-critical thought today, I will replace it with a kind thought.*

Sunday: *Self-compassion is the magic ingredient in my recovery today.*

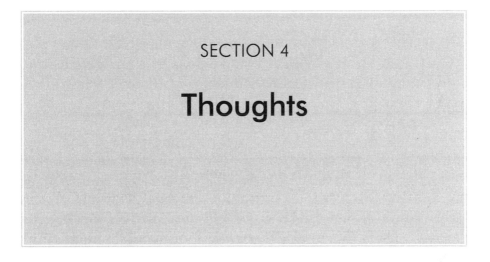

SECTION 4

Thoughts

16

Minding Your Mind

*Leave your front door and your backdoor open. Allow your
thoughts to come and go. Just don't serve them tea.*

—**Shunryu Suzuki**

In London, when the subway train stops, a sign reminds passengers to
"Mind the gap," so as to step safely off the train. It's a gentle reminder to
bring awareness to that moment and notice what you're doing, so you
don't get hurt.

In recovery, it's a very good idea to *Mind your mind.*

Much like watching your step, watching your thoughts can keep you
from stumbling. It can protect you from a potentially dangerous fall.
Recovering mindfully has a lot to do with balance, and there is nothing
that can send you off-balance faster than your mind. Thinking tends to
get stuck in really unhelpful negative, repetitive patterns, and negative
thoughts cause a lot of harm. They lead to relationship troubles, bad
moods, bad decisions, and stress. They lay the groundwork for unhappi-
ness, hopelessness, and relapse. If you can become aware of these negative thoughts and change them for the better, everything else can change
for the better, too.

Remember this simple phrase for balancing your thoughts: "Catch it,
check it, change it" (Burns 2008). You can learn to change unhelpful
thinking patterns by noticing them, figuring out whether or not they are
true, and then changing them to something that's more helpful. This
chapter will help you get started by learning how to *catch* your thoughts.
Noticing what your mind is up to is important in your recovery. Because,
let's face it, it is easy to lose your balance when you aren't paying
attention.

Through your mindfulness practice over time, you will become more aware of what's happening in your head. But let's assume for the moment that you don't always know what thoughts are racing through your mind. Maybe they move too fast, or maybe you're not used to noticing them. It's hard to catch them. If you have been living with addiction, it may be extra hard to see what's going on in your own mind. Denial and other defense mechanisms (ways you tried to protect yourself from emotional pain while you were addicted) make it hard to see your mind clearly. And if you are just beginning to recover, your brain may feel hazy. Trying to catch your thoughts may feel like searching for street signs in a fog—that haze will clear more and more over time, so don't lose hope! As with everything you are learning, give yourself some gentle compassion as you practice observing your thoughts.

One great way to catch your thoughts is to start with your mood, because certain thoughts are often lurking behind your mood. And sometimes you may not be aware that your mind is up to no good until suddenly you aren't feeling any good. So if you notice yourself becoming stressed, irritable, sad, fearful, or frustrated…that's a good time to pause. Take a slow, deep breath. Turn your attention to your mind. See if you can pinpoint what was happening and what you were thinking about when your sudden shift in mood arose.

For example, if you recalled that *Richard just walked by without saying hello*, you may have thought, *He is still mad about the other day.* And that would be one way of explaining it. That is one possible interpretation of what happened. You also might have thought, *He must be really out of it today.* That is another possible interpretation of what happened. Every situation or event in our lives is up for interpretation. The way you make sense of what happens is through your thoughts. However, if you can come up with only one possible explanation for something, you are probably stuck in unbalanced thinking!

That's a trap. Your mind is keeping you off-balance, and you may be headed for a fall. Mind your mind!

Give yourself plenty of practice. Take the time to meditate and quietly observe your thoughts. While the goal of meditation may be to quiet the chatter of the mind, it can also be used to notice and observe the mind at work. Approach your thoughts with calm curiosity. Your thoughts are a lot like forest creatures. They are skittish. If you are loud and busy, they will flee to the trees, out of sight. Sit quietly. Be peaceful and patient. Wait. If they feel safe, your thoughts will reveal themselves to you. Remember, what you are doing is profound and powerful. It is the first step in rebalancing your thoughts, and this is the gateway to joyful, balanced recovery.

Exercise: Minding-Your-Mind Meditation

Choose a quiet place to rest without distractions. Lie flat on your back or sit in a comfortable position, whichever is better for relaxing over the next few minutes. Once you are comfortable, close your eyes. Take several deep, cleansing breaths to bring yourself into this space and this moment. Now imagine your mind is a cloudless sky. You are peaceful and serene as you gaze at it. Breathe deeply and enjoy the vast blue emptiness. Take the time to notice its color. Does the blue change shades as you gaze at it?

As you rest quietly, notice how new thoughts appear in the mind. Let each thought form clearly, like skywriting on that backdrop of blue. Notice each thought as it appears. Read it, and then see how the letters begin to fade. Each thought slowly floats away. A new thought appears, fluffy and white against the blue. See each thought clearly, but do not follow it as it floats away. Let each thought pass. Notice what shows up in the mind, knowing that none of it is permanent. Enjoy the calm, peaceful sky.

Affirmations for Minding Your Mind

We recommend you say these affirmations out loud throughout the day to connect with your intention of a mindful recovery. We also recommend you type one affirmation into your smartphone each morning as a reminder to use it three to five times daily. You can download a printable copy of these affirmations at the website for this book: http://www.newharbinger.com/40705.

Monday: *I am not my thoughts.*

Tuesday: *I observe my thoughts and see them clearly.*

Wednesday: *I am practicing minding my mind. With practice, I can see what my mind is up to.*

Thursday: *I notice my thoughts, without judgment.*

Friday: *I calmly watch my thoughts.*

Saturday: *My thoughts are interpretations, not facts.*

Sunday: *When a feeling arises, I pause and look to my mind.*

17
Changing Your Thoughts

You become what you think about all day long.

—Ralph Waldo Emerson

There is a great saying in recovery from addiction: "I'm not responsible for my first thought. I am responsible for my second." Your thoughts might show up automatically, but in your recovery, you can change the way that you think.

Most of us assume our mind is right. We don't spend a lot of time questioning it. But if there is one thing worth learning in life, it is that your thoughts are not facts. Thoughts are interpretations; they are *judgments*. In mindfulness, we attempt to move away from judgment, but it isn't easy to do. The best we can do is to keep our thoughts as realistic and helpful as possible. Your mind tries to be helpful by offering countless thoughts and interpretations, and a lot of them are *not* helpful to you. Stop trusting every thought that your mind generates! It is time to put yourself in charge of deciding which thought is helpful and which thought is not.

In the previous chapter, you learned the handy phrase "Catch it, check it, change it" for managing the unhelpful thoughts that can lead you off track. You learned the importance of minding your mind. With practice, you are becoming a skilled observer and catching your thoughts as they arise. The next steps are to *check* your thoughts and to *change* them.

As you check your thoughts and recognize that some are not completely true, you can develop new ways of thinking. You can change your thinking and see the world in a whole new way. Calm, balanced, and realistic thinking leads to stable emotions, happy relationships, wise decisions, and healthy recovery from addiction.

Use the next exercise regularly to check and change unbalanced, unhelpful thoughts. If you find it especially hard to check or to change your thoughts, it's a good idea to have a counselor or therapist help you. Invite someone you trust to help you see your thoughts clearly and change them effectively. Joyful recovery begins with your mind!

Exercise: Checking the Evidence

Find a quiet and comfortable place to sit with your journal. Take notes in your journal throughout this exercise, as writing will slow down your thoughts and make them clear. Center yourself first by focusing on your breath. Be present for this experience. Thank your mind for all that it offers you and all the ways it tries to help you.

Now choose a situation that is troubling to you. On a scale of intensity from 1 to 10, this situation should be troubling you at about a level 5: not too intense but problematic enough that it is worth exploring.

Catch your thoughts about this situation by asking: *How do I explain the situation to myself? How am I making sense of this situation?* Once you catch a thought, ask yourself: *What evidence do I have that this is true? What evidence is there that this might not be completely true?* As an example, consider the situation in which your friend Richard walked by without saying hello, and you thought, *He is still mad about the other day.* Now, ask yourself, how do you know this is true? Is there some evidence that it might not be completely true? For example, after your argument the other day, Richard called up to say he was sorry for what happened, and you made plans to get together next week.

If you have no evidence for a thought being true or if you have some evidence that it might be false, then consider whether it may be an unhelpful thought. Note that unhelpful, automatic thought patterns tend to have certain qualities. Check if your thought is

- Negative

- Jumping to conclusions or making assumptions

- Judgmental

- Limited (as if there were only one way of seeing things)

- Based on a *stuck belief* leftover from childhood instead of how you choose to see the world as an adult

- Driven by emotion rather than by a mix of emotion and logic

If you find that a thought is negative, limited, or driven by old beliefs or emotions, it is time to make a change. Practice changing your thoughts now by asking yourself: *What positives can I see in this situation that might balance out the negatives? What other ways can I interpret this situation?* Find at least two new ways to see the situation. For example, in the case of Richard walking by without talking to you, is there another way of explaining what happened? Could he have just been out of it today? Is it possible he didn't even see you? Write down at least two new ways of seeing the situation. You have just checked and changed your thinking.

Now do this with two other situations that have been troubling you.

Note that the qualities of balanced thoughts include curiosity, open-mindedness, and optimism. Balanced thinking *wonders* about things; it is compassionate rather than critical. Balanced thoughts are based on facts and evidence rather than on emotions or preconceived notions. Even if you have decided your thoughts are generally completely balanced and realistic, it's good to practice looking at things in a new way. See how many different interpretations you can come up with whenever your thinking seems stuck in old unhelpful ways of looking at things.

This is hard work, but it is worth it. You are strong enough to stand up to unhelpful, off-balance thoughts that keep you stuck. You are recovering, and you are ready to change your life!

Affirmations for Changing Your Thoughts

We recommend you say these affirmations out loud throughout the day to connect with your intention of a mindful recovery. We also recommend you type one affirmation into your smartphone each morning as a reminder to use it three to five times daily. You can download a printable copy of these affirmations at the website for this book: http://www .newharbinger.com/40705.

Monday: *I am not responsible for my first thought; I am responsible for my second.*

Tuesday: *I understand that my thoughts are not facts.*

Wednesday: *I can change my thoughts, and by changing my thoughts, I change my life.*

Thursday: *I will receive only realistic, balanced, and helpful ways of thinking.*

Friday: *I choose which thoughts are helpful and which thoughts it is time to change.*

Saturday: *There are many ways of seeing each situation; I choose to see things in a clear and balanced way.*

Sunday: *In recovery, I take charge of my thinking; I free myself from unhelpful thoughts.*

18

Tricky Addiction Thinking

*The real voyage of discovery consists not in seeking
landscapes, but in having new eyes.*

—Marcel Proust

Even in recovery, it is important to understand the addicted mind.
Understanding your addiction is empowering; it helps you to release
shame and take control of your recovery. And in the early months of
recovery, addicted thinking can continue and cause relapse. So take
some time now to understand your addicted mind.

Addicts are some of the most intelligent people we have ever met.
Unfortunately, the fabulous brains addicts possess have been stolen by
the addiction. It's like when the bad guy in the movie gets ahold of the
good guy's magic wand. Trouble is bound to ensue when all that power is
in the wrong hands.

What kind of trouble can happen? Well that once healthy active
mind has now devoted itself to justifying, rationalizing, and romanticiz-
ing the addictive behavior. The addicted mind may spend a fair amount
of time trying to find a way out of this mess, too. But because the addiction has taken over the controls, the mind usually succumbs to the dark
side. The addicted mind creates powerful explanations for how and why
to keep on using. It is so darn clever, in fact, that it can use the desire to
stop using as a reason to use: *If I stop before I'm really ready, it won't stick.
I'll only drink and smoke a little weed; it doesn't make sense to stop everything
at once. Or I will stop the day after my birthday, when the timing is right.*

Notice how logical these statements sound? These ideas are clever
enough to seem true. And maybe they are—sometimes, for some people,
under certain circumstances. But for the most part, these ideas put a

space between you and recovery. Escaping from your addiction has just been put off until tomorrow or until next month, or until some hypothetical time that will feel "right." That day never comes, and the addicted mind has kept you trapped again. And again. And again.

The better you get at knowing the tricks of the addicted mind, the better you can defend yourself against relapse. You won't fall for its lies. Putting off recovery is one of your mind's many tricks. Let's consider some others.

Making the Addiction Sound Like a Treat

Thoughts like these include *I've had such a bad day. I deserve it. At the end of a stressful week, I should get to unwind. Everybody needs one vice. I work hard; I can play hard.*

In this case, your mind turns things completely upside down by telling you that your addiction is a reward and a sign of self-respect. It says engaging in your addiction means you are free and living well. Hogwash! Your addiction is a cage.

There is nothing rewarding about being addicted. You don't show respect to yourself by relapsing; it is crippling to your self-esteem. Yes, everyone needs and deserves to unwind and have a treat now and then. But your addiction was probably not just now and then. And there is nothing relaxing or fulfilling about being an addict!

The Illusion of Control

The illusion of control is an extremely common line of thinking. It's when your addicted mind tries to tell you that you're not actually an addict, or that maybe you were one but you're definitely not anymore. It starts creating a new story about how you actually have the power to control your addictive behavior. A cleanse, a detox, a little clean time, a new spiritual guru, a solid plan for not overdoing it, other people to make sure you stay in line...your addicted mind has a lot of reasons for how things will be different this time. You might recognize thoughts like *I'll only have one. This is the last time. It's only for this special occasion. I know better now. I finally see things clearly, and now I can control myself.* Or *I will stop again tomorrow.* Oh, your tricky addicted mind! Of course, you want to feel like you are in control. And you are in control—of your recovery. You get to make healthy decisions in your recovery. You get to chart a course for your own life. But you were not in control of your addiction. You chose to recover for a reason. *I'll just have one* is an illusion of control.

Give yourself a dose of truth. You probably tried for a long time to control your addictive behavior. You tried to make it work. You have all the evidence you need: it wasn't different before, and it won't be different this time. Don't take the bait!

Audio for the next meditation exercise is available at http://www .newharbinger.com/40705.

Exercise 1: Calling Forth the Strong, Recovering Self

We suggest that you do this brief meditation daily if you are in the first six months of your recovery, and continue to practice it any time the addicted mind generates one of the thoughts above.

Find a peaceful space, alone with your thoughts. Sit quietly, with eyes closed, and turn your attention to your breath. Use your breath to release tension from your body and bring you into the present moment. Your attention may wander away, and that's okay. Gently invite your attention back to this moment, back to this process.

When you find yourself in a moment of calm reflection, ask your recovering self to step forward. Ask it to be strong. Ask it to take charge. Call upon your recovering self to see whether the addicted mind is up to its tricks and not to be swayed by it today. Repeat these phrases to yourself for as long as it feels right to you:

I dwell in truth. I see the truth. I choose the truth. In this wisdom, I recover.

Exercise 2: Finding Your True Treats

If your mind is making the addiction sound like a treat, it is time to make some changes. Take out your journal, and take some time to make a list of truly soothing, exciting, and otherwise pleasurable treats you can give yourself. Choose things that empower and uplift you instead of things that cut you down. You do deserve good things. You deserve a lot better than the misery that is waiting for you in a relapse!

Exercise 3: Seeing Through the Illusion of Control

If your mind is tossing out illusion-of-control thoughts, take charge by getting honest with yourself. In your journal, make a list of all the ways you tried to control your addictive behavior. Be honest with yourself as you answer the following questions:

- How well did it work to control your addiction?

- How did your addiction look (over the long run)?

- How much time and energy did you spend on trying to manage your addictive behavior?

Being honest with yourself will stop your addicted mind from tricking you out of all that recovery has to offer!

Affirmations to Counter Tricky Addiction Thinking

We recommend you say these affirmations out loud throughout the day to connect with your intention of a mindful recovery. We also recommend you type one affirmation into your smartphone each morning as a reminder to use it three to five times daily. You can download a printable copy of these affirmations at the website for this book: http://www .newharbinger.com/40705.

Monday: *I do not fall for the tricks of my addiction.*

Tuesday: *I am free from my addiction and will not be trapped again.*

Wednesday: *My addicted mind may lie to me, but I can see the truth.*

Thursday: *I cultivate gratitude each day of my recovery.*

Friday: *My old ways of thinking will no longer keep me stuck.*

Saturday: *I choose actions that fulfill me as treats and rewards.*

Sunday: *I respect myself, and I deserve good things.*

19

Tricky Recovery Thinking

Simply allow your thoughts and experience to come and go,
without ever grasping at them.

—Dilgo Khyentse Rinpoche

The addicted brain is sneaky and sketchy. It is full of tricks for keeping you in the addicted trap. But even when you find your way free of that trap, you've still got to pay attention. The recovering mind has some tricks of its own! Its two main ways of messing with you are by minimizing the consequences of your addiction and by making it seem like your recovery is no fun. Let's take a closer look at these two tricky thinking patterns.

Making Light of the Consequences

There's a saying in Alcoholics Anonymous: "The further I get from my last drink, the closer I get to my next one." Getting some recovery time under your belt absolutely makes life easier—your triggers will get weaker, and the problems your addiction caused will start to smooth out—but in an unhappy twist of events, getting some clean time can also set you up for relapse, because your recovering brain has a very suspect memory of events. One of its shady tricks is to forget how much misery your addiction was causing you. Over time, the painful feelings fade just enough to make your addictive behavior seem less risky. Feeling better, you start wondering if maybe things weren't really so bad. If you start to have thoughts like *What's the big deal? I never drank as much as so-and-so,* or *Maybe I didn't need to stop completely*—as if getting into recovery were just an overreaction of some kind—watch out! Your recovering mind is not letting you remember what it was really like.

Give yourself a dose of truth. You got into recovery for a reason! Even if it was at the urging of people who love you, that means there was probably a lot of conflict in your relationships. Maybe that was reason enough to change your behaviors. And besides, no one can make you do something you really don't want to do. You must have had your own reasons for making this change. If you are very honest with yourself (and can quiet those tricky addictive thoughts), you will remember why recovery became a priority in your life.

Thinking That Recovery Is the Pits

Thinking that recovery is the pits is the addicted mind trying to convince you that recovery and all the hard work you are doing to recover aren't worth it. Thoughts like this include: *I'm so sick of these meetings, I never get to have fun anymore, Other people don't have to do all this stuff, why should I?* and *Nobody gives me credit for everything I'm doing.* These thoughts can be summed up as *sobriety sucks.* It's a pattern of thinking that is dangerous and faulty. Your mind wants to chase you back to your addictive behavior.

Remember what's true. You can be proud of yourself for doing the hard work of recovering. Your loved ones support you. You can see light at the end of the tunnel. Even when recovery is hard, it's probably not harder than waking up every day in your addiction. You had bad days and difficult feelings when you were using, too, but instead of knowing these days and feelings would pass, you were driven further into your addiction, and you couldn't see a way out. You mostly felt shame and fear. Your loved ones were walking away. There was only a big black hole at the end of the tunnel.

If you are finding it especially hard to break out of negative thinking about recovery, consider talking to a counselor or a therapist about your feelings. Depression can be common in the first eighteen months of recovery from addiction and can happen later, and depression is notorious for not allowing you to see clearly. You might need some support to see what's good in your life.

Take some time to get familiar with the tricks of your recovering mind. Complete the following exercises to take charge of those pesky thoughts!

Exercise 1: Why You Decided to Recover

Sit quietly with your journal. Begin by breathing deeply with your eyes closed. Give yourself a few minutes to become relaxed and centered. As you become more peaceful, set an intention to be guided toward honesty and clarity in this moment.

Make a list of the reasons you decided to recover. What was happening with your family, friends, work, hobbies, finances, and health as a result of your addiction? What was your addiction stealing from you? Consider times you felt ashamed, frightened, worried, regretful, and frustrated in your addiction. Write as many reasons as you can think of, big and small, for why you decided to change your life.

Exercise 2: Your Gratitude List

If *recovering is the pits* thoughts are haunting you, make yourself a gratitude list. Using your journal, write down as many things as you can think of that you are grateful for. It can be as simple as enjoying a hot cup of coffee or waking up clearheaded in the morning. Continue working on this list as a nightly practice every evening before bed, writing down five reasons that you are grateful.

Affirmations to Combat Tricky Recovery Thinking

We recommend you say these affirmations out loud throughout the day to connect with your intention of a mindful recovery. We also recommend you type one affirmation into your smartphone each morning as a reminder to use it three to five times daily. You can download a printable copy of these affirmations at the website for this book: http://www .newharbinger.com/40705.

Monday: *I had hard days in my addiction; I accept that I will have hard days in my recovery, too. I move through my challenges.*

Tuesday: *I am grateful for my recovery.*

Wednesday: *I remember why I chose to recover.*

Thursday: *Recovery brings good into my life, today and in the future.*

Friday: *My recovery is a priority, because it's worth it.*

Saturday: *A clean and sober life is full of countless rewards.*

Sunday: *I choose a healthy, happy life.*

20

The Inner Bully

I would like my life to be a statement of love and compassion—
and where it isn't, that's where my work lies.

—Ram Dass

He picks on your haircut, your clothes, and your complexion. She laughs when you make a mistake. He questions your choices. She tells you that you'll fail.

Man, oh man, is it awful to be bullied. It feels pretty terrible to be picked on or pushed around. It might make you want to stay under the covers and hide. It might make you want to scream. It might make you want to use. Anyone would tell you it's best to stay away from bullies. But the sad truth is that most of us have a bully that lives in our own minds.

The *inner bully* is that judgmental voice in your head that cuts you down. It loves to tell you what you are doing wrong in your life or how the problems you are facing are your fault or how other people are better than you. This voice picks away at your self-esteem, sometimes all day.

As you recover from addiction, as you heal and move forward, you are going to encounter this harsh self-critic. Use these strategies to take the power away from your inner bully and gift the power back to yourself.

Separate from the bully. There's a saying: "The last thing a fish will notice is the water." If you are swimming around all day in self-critical thoughts, you may not even realize it. The first step is to realize *I am being bullied.* The bully is not you; it's a collection of old nasty energies that others have projected onto you throughout your life. Things that were said to you, mean ways you were treated, experiences of trauma, hurt, shame, or neglect—they have taken shape as this bully. Our experiences really do mold us, especially as children, and the negative stuff gets in. Notice what the bully is up to.

Tune out the bully. Maybe somebody told you once that if you ignore a bully, the bully will eventually give up and leave you alone. Sometimes ignoring a bully—even the one in your own mind—will only empower it. But sometimes tuning it out will lead to less torment. When you notice your inner bully at work, refocus your energies on positive things like recovery behaviors and helpful self-talk. Distract yourself with something you enjoy. Your inner bully may just give up and go away.

Talk to your bully. Some bullies don't back down until you stand up to them. When the name-calling begins or the bully second-guesses your every move, say *That's enough.* Your inner bully may be used to ranting and raving at you without interruption. Standing up to it will probably catch your bully off guard. Tell it to *Stop picking on me.* Or say that *Your words hurt. I don't want to hear from you anymore!*

Approach your bully with curiosity. Another way to deal with a bully—and quite a powerful way—is to approach it with love. Bring along your mindful curiosity and compassion. Next time your inner bully is picking on you, ask it why: *Gosh, you're really coming after me today. What's going on?* Check in with yourself to see if you are in need of some extra support. Maybe it's time for some encouragement from a friend? Maybe you need a snack? A break from work? Give yourself the patience and kindness you deserve; your bully might just melt away when you show yourself some love!

Live in the moment. Present-moment awareness is the key to so much. In the case of the inner bully, living in the moment may silence it completely. The bully in your mind thrives on comparison. When you are in the present and experiencing nonjudgmental awareness, the inner bully cannot exist (Bays 2009). When the inner bully starts its squawking, breathe deeply and bring yourself back to the here and now. Use your five senses. Engage any or all of your senses with your full attention.

Managing your inner bully is going to take time and practice. But it is so very worth the work. You deserve to be treated with kindness and respect!

Exercise: Calming Your Inner Bully

Find a quiet place to meditate and bring yourself some comforts. You might bring a hot cup of tea, a soft blanket, or an object you associate with happy times. With your comforts nearby, sit peacefully and close your eyes. Breathe deeply with a smooth, slow give-and-take between the inhale and the exhale. Using your breath as your guide, ground yourself in this moment. You can always return to the breath. It is always there for you.

Once you are feeling present and tranquil, begin to contemplate your inner bully. What arises in this space? What do you see? What is it saying to you?

We know the bully can be scary. You have your comforts here with you any time you need some support. Maybe you will have a sip of tea, paying close attention to the sensations that occur as you hold the mug in your hand and feel the liquid warm your mouth, throat, and stomach. Maybe you will gently rub your blanket with your fingers, noticing its textures and the warmth it provides. Maybe you will hold your special object in your hands for a moment and offer gratitude for the joy it brings you.

Take as much time as you need to remember that you are safe and loved. Then revisit your inner bully. Practice the strategies for calming the bully that were suggested earlier in this chapter. Which strategies seem to quiet the bully today? Feel safe to experiment with these strategies for as long as you like, knowing that taking the power back from your bully may take a while, and that's okay. You are exactly where you need to be.

Affirmations to Quiet Your Inner Bully

We recommend you say these affirmations out loud throughout the day to connect with your intention of a mindful recovery. We also recommend you type one affirmation into your smartphone each morning as a reminder to use it three to five times daily. You can download a printable copy of these affirmations at the website for this book: http://www.newharbinger.com/40705.

Monday: *My inner bully is not all of me.*

Tuesday: *I take the power away from my inner bully. I find my true voice.*

Wednesday: *Today I ignore my inner bully; it does not deserve my beautiful attention.*

Thursday: *Today I stand up to my inner bully; I will not let it push me around.*

Friday: *I deserve loving-kindness without exception.*

Saturday: *I am learning that wisdom and truth are to be found deep within me.*

Sunday: *The inner bully cannot dwell where I dwell. I dwell in the here and now.*

21
Positive Thinking

How you live today is how you live your life.

—Tara Brach

Seeing life in a positive light is a powerful step toward happy, healthy recovery from addiction.

But thinking positively isn't easy. These days we all are practically programmed to see things in a negative light. Advertisements crash into us constantly, announcing that we need some new thing or experience, implying that until we get that thing or experience, life won't be good enough. Social media keeps us comparing ourselves with each other, and we always seem to come up short. And the news? Well, it is scaring the heck out of us. Through the lens of our TV, the world looks crazy, and the future looks bleak.

It isn't easy, but you can see your way clear of all this negativity. You can think positively, if you are willing to pause and let what's positive come into view. You can create a more positive outlook in recovery today and every day with these strategies.

Begin with gratitude. Mahatma Gandhi told us we must be the change we wish to see in the world (Gandhi 1993). If you want a more positive world, you must be your most positive self, so create a nightly gratitude list of five things you are thankful for. On days that this feels difficult, consider what you have that others do not have—maybe a bed or blanket, a friend, twenty-four hours of sobriety, or the ability to see. Once you can recognize what is good in your life, you can cultivate a more positive overall outlook.

Engage with nature. Nature has an incredible capacity to soothe, invigorate, and sustain you. Many holistic practitioners suggest placing your bare feet in grass, dirt, or sand for thirty minutes per day to improve well-being. Even if you can spend only five minutes with a potted plant, connect with nature. Be present, use all of your senses, and experience the positivity.

Be your own cheerleader. Gifting yourself with positive self-talk is a fantastic way to increase your positive thoughts. Try phrases such as *I can do this, I will find my way, Everything will turn out okay, It's okay to make mistakes sometimes,* or *I can accept myself exactly as I am today.* If this is tricky, think about how you would talk to someone you love. If your best friend lost his job, what would you say to lift his spirits? If your child got hurt, how would you comfort her?

There's one thing to remember, though. Being positive doesn't mean forgetting what's real and true. It might sound positive if you said to yourself, *I am strong and doing great, so I'm sure I can handle one beer!* But that would be the addicted mind using positive thinking as one of its tricks. Don't trust any thoughts that put you at risk for relapse.

You have choices about how you think about your world, about others, and about yourself. If you want greater joy, peace, and connection in your recovery, choose to be positive!

Audio for the next meditation exercise is available at http://www .newharbinger.com/40705.

Exercise: Enlisting Your Cheering Section

If it feels especially hard to talk to yourself in a positive way, it might be time to enlist some support through visualization. This meditation can be practiced at any time.

Take several quiet minutes for yourself, choosing a comfortable and peaceful place to sit with eyes closed. Breathe deeply and allow your body to relax. Once you feel relaxed and present, begin to visualize the people in your life who support you. Visualize the people who have lifted you up. Only the people who truly help you feel good about yourself or have done so in the past are welcome here. Invite only helpful thoughts, feelings, and images into this space.

Close your eyes and really see these people. Watch and see that they are all taking their seats together in your cheering section. One by one, they wave to you and take a seat. Some blow kisses; some grin at you. Continue to think about everyone and anyone who have been a supportive presence in your life. Whether it is large or small, watch how your cheering section fills up.

Now, see these people begin to cheer for you. One by one, they are calling out, "We're with you!" "I know it's hard work, but you're doing great!" "You've got this!" "You can do it!" "We've got your back!" "I'm so proud of you!" "Keep up the good work!" "You are even stronger than you think!" "I'm on your side!" "We are here if you need us!"

Continue to imagine your own supportive phrases for them to shout. See them applauding for you, maybe rising to their feet for a standing ovation. Realize that you can call on this cheering section whenever you like. It's always there for you!

Affirmations for Positive Thinking

We recommend you say these affirmations out loud throughout the day to connect with your intention of a mindful recovery. We also recommend you type one affirmation into your smartphone each morning as a reminder to use it three to five times daily. You can download a printable copy of these affirmations at the website for this book: http://www .newharbinger.com/40705.

Monday: *I nourish myself with positive thoughts today.*

Tuesday: *I have a choice about how I think. I choose my positive thoughts today.*

Wednesday: *Today I will be the change I wish to see in the world.*

Thursday: *My recovery includes permission to change negative thoughts to positive ones.*

Friday: *Today I will notice and reflect on five reasons I have to be grateful.*

Saturday: *Whenever I need a boost today, I can listen to the cheers from my cheering section.*

Sunday: *I create my life in recovery, and I choose to think positive thoughts.*

22

Racing Thoughts

Patience is also a form of action.

—**Auguste Rodin**

Assuming you have a brain—and unless you are the scarecrow from the Land of Oz, that's a pretty safe assumption—you have probably experienced racing thoughts. Racing thoughts are when your mind is so active it seems almost impossible to slow it down. Your thoughts jump and fly in all directions, sending you bouncing from idea to idea, worry to worry, stress to stress. Your mind is like a bag of microwaveable popcorn when it really gets cooking. *Pop, pow, bang.* If left unattended, those kernels can start smoking pretty quickly!

One of the biggest challenges in recovery is finding new ways to quiet the mind, because chances are you used to use your addiction to accomplish that. Your addictive behavior may have been the one thing that seemed to quiet those thoughts and slow the world back down to a reasonable pace. It worked—for a while. But then your addictive behavior turned on you. It made your life chaotic, and chaos is a recipe for racing thoughts. Now it is time to try something new. You can manage those racing thoughts in a healthy way.

Racing thoughts may be troubling to you in recovery, but hang in there! You are cultivating a mindful way of life. A more peaceful mind is bound to follow.

Most of the time, relaxation and meditation techniques are soothing to our bodies and minds. But some of the time, these methods can actually make us more anxious and uncomfortable. If your mind races through relaxation or meditation exercises, the following grounding techniques are a helpful alternative; these techniques are inspired by practices in *Seeking Safety: A Treatment Manual for PTSD and Substance Abuse*, by Dr. Lisa M. Najavits (2001).

Notice the space you are in. If you are sitting, touch your chair. What material is it made of? Is it hard or soft? Is it warm or cold? If you are lying in bed, touch your mattress and pillow. Find an object that is nearby, and pick it up. Explore it closely as if you were seeing it for the first time. Notice its colors, its shape, its temperature, and how light or heavy it feels in your hand. If you didn't know what this object was called, what name would you give it?

Notice the room you are in. How many different colors can you find in this room? How many things can you find that are blue? How about brown?

Play a little trivia game with yourself. Name as many states in the United States as you can. Now name as many animals as you can that begin with the letter R. How about animals that start with the letter A? How many movies have you seen that star Tom Hanks? Or Meryl Streep? Or Denzel Washington? Or your favorite actor?

Remember your favorite things. What is your favorite sports team? How about your favorite player? Imagine that player smiling after winning the big game. What is your favorite song to dance to? Try to remember the words to that song. Hum or sing it to yourself. Think about your favorite funny sitcom. Who is your favorite character? What is your favorite season? Think of all the reasons you enjoy that time of year. What is your favorite color? Imagine a bubble of this color gently surrounding and soothing you. You can float comfortably in that bubble for as long as you like; whenever you decide to pop the bubble, the color simply disappears. You are here in this room, safe and sound in this moment.

After you try any or all of these grounding techniques, notice how you feel. If your mind is still racing, feel free to begin again. If your thoughts have quieted a bit and you feel more relaxed, that's great. You can revisit these techniques at any time. They are always available to you.

Exercise: Managing Racing Thoughts

Racing thoughts often occur at certain times, and you are more likely to have racing thoughts when you are bored, when you are trying to get something done, or when you want to go to sleep. Use the grounding techniques suggested earlier, or manage your racing thoughts with these strategies designed for certain circumstances.

What to do when you are bored and have racing thoughts. Engage your brain with something challenging to you physically or mentally. It will force your mind to focus. The trick is to find something that interests you and is difficult enough to require focus but not so difficult that your racing mind will give up and wander off. You could do a crossword puzzle or try sprinting as fast as you can go. It is very hard to stay in the present moment when your mind is racing, but doing a task that requires focus may slow down your mind enough to get you back to the present. Then it's up to you to practice your mindfulness skills. Bring your full attention to whatever you are doing in that moment.

What to do about racing thoughts during work or tasks. If you are trying to get something done and racing thoughts are getting in the way, take a break and engage with nature. There is something incredibly healing about spending time outdoors. If cold weather is a problem, bundle up! At least get yourself a few good deep breaths of fresh air. Feel the sun on your skin.

What to do about racing thoughts at bedtime. Having racing thoughts at bedtime is a common problem. Use a consistent bedtime routine to train your body and mind to slow down. It's important to create a gap between the rushed, hectic world of your day and the quiet, restful world of a good night's sleep. You can also try a guided meditation before going to bed. Lots of websites and apps offer meditations.

You can quiet your racing thoughts!

Affirmations to Quell Racing Thoughts

We recommend you say these affirmations out loud throughout the day to connect with your intention of a mindful recovery. We also recommend you type one affirmation into your smartphone each morning as a reminder to use it three to five times daily. You can download a printable copy of these affirmations at the website for this book: http://www.newharbinger.com/40705.

Monday: *I have many healthy ways to quiet my mind.*

Tuesday: *I ground myself in the here and now. In this moment, all is well.*

Wednesday: *I detach from my mind and tune in to my body. My body is present in the here and now.*

Thursday: *I enjoy challenging my body and mind; I find clarity and calm in moments of challenge.*

Friday: *I embrace nature and all the ways that it heals me.*

Saturday: *Today I stand tall and plant my feet on the ground. Just like a tree, I am strong and connected to the earth.*

Sunday: *I guide and focus my thoughts where I want them to go.*

The Gift of Recovery

SECTION 5

Cravings and Triggers

23

Awareness of Triggers

If you notice anything, it leads you to notice more and more.

—Mary Oliver

Tom always smoked pot after a fight with his wife. Now even a little argument with her makes him think about using. Stella and her sister always used meth together. Now Stella finds herself feeling restless around her sister. Miguel bought his beer at the market near his house. Buying groceries there or even driving past it is a challenge in his recovery. Lizzie went to the casino on paydays. Now whenever she has money in her pocket, the urge to gamble comes on fast.

These people are experiencing triggers. To put it simply, a *trigger* can be any person, place, thing, situation, or feeling that appeared alongside or right before your addictive behavior. These things become so connected to your addiction that when you encounter them in recovery, they trigger a *craving*, or a desire, for the thing that you associate with them. Everyone has his or her own set of triggers. The more you know about yours, the better off you will be.

Thinking triggers. Even a passing thought of engaging in your addiction can be a trigger. Allowing those thoughts to build up is especially likely to cause cravings. In fact, imagining yourself engaging in your addictive behavior makes cravings especially intense. This can easily lead to relapse if you're not mindful.

Feeling triggers. Emotions are often what drive people to their addictive behavior. You may have used when you were angry, when you were happy and celebrating, when you were lonely, or when you were scared. Now those feelings create an urge to use. Things you see, smell, or hear can also be feeling triggers, such as the smell of alcohol or the sound of a beer can opening.

Behavioral triggers. Certain behaviors can be triggers, such as going to bars, answering a text from your dealer, spending time with using friends, walking through the liquor aisle at your local grocery store, or buying your favorite wine "for the party."

Social triggers. Social triggers are the people and social situations connected to your addiction. We know these people may be important to you. It can be hard to think about them as triggers when you really see them as loved ones. They can be both. Be honest with yourself about what's what. You can handle things however you choose, but you get the power of choice only if you let yourself see things clearly.

Exercise 1: Identifying Your Triggers

In your journal, list as many of your triggers as you can think of. Ask yourself what people, places, things, emotions, smells, sounds, sights, and situations are connected to your addiction. The list should be long!

Next, looking at each trigger on the list, decide which triggers you should always avoid. The triggers you should always avoid if you used drugs will probably be any drug-using situations (you can avoid these, and there are probably no good reasons to engage with them). The same goes for casinos if you are a gambling addict or for strip clubs if you are a sex addict. Label these situations and your former dealer or other people who encourage your addictive behavior as triggers to "always avoid."

Next, if you decide you would like to reengage at some point with an avoidable trigger, label it "avoid until..." and then be very specific about how you will know when it's safe to expose yourself to this trigger;

also write down and be specific about ways you will keep yourself safe in your recovery for the first few exposures. For example, you might avoid drinking situations completely until you have at least ninety days of sobriety and have established a great support system. Then you may decide to bring a sober buddy with you to the first of several events where alcohol is served. Make a solid plan about how you will deal with triggers that arise.

Finally, label any unavoidable triggers (such as feeling bored, a certain look your spouse gives you, getting into your car, or the sound of a text message) with the word "cope." These unavoidable triggers are the ones you must deal with, and the next exercise will help you with that.

Exercise 2: Creating a Coping Kit

It is time to create your personal coping kit! This is something you can reach for whenever a trigger shows up and then use its contents to ground yourself in the present moment. You might choose to keep your coping kit in your car, on your nightstand, or under your desk at work. You can also make more than one kit. The kit contains objects that will engage your five senses, things that make you feel good, and some words of encouragement.

To create your coping kit, collect some or all of the following:

- Pictures that engage you visually, such as beautiful scenes from nature

- Perfume samples or a paper towel or tissue sprayed with perfume

- A tea bag with a nice smell or a scented candle

- A stone, coin, or other small object you can hold in your hand

- Something very soft, like a piece of a blanket, a cotton ball, or a feather

- Something with an interesting texture, like a piece of sandpaper or a ball of tin foil

- Items with vibrant and engaging colors

- Chewing gum, breath mints, or a piece of chocolate

- A piece of bubble wrap to pop

- A small rattle or jar with pebbles inside

- Pictures from magazines that remind you of the life you really want

- Notecards with your favorite quotes, prayers, or mantras

- A *reality card*, which lists the real consequences of your addiction and reasons you are choosing to recover

You may be able to create your kit from items you have in your house. Or it may feel good to go to an art supply store or other places to find exactly what you want for your kit. Why not treat it as a scavenger hunt? Have some fun with creating your very own coping kit!

Affirmations for Awareness of Triggers

We recommend you say these affirmations out loud throughout the day to connect with your intention of a mindful recovery. We also recommend you type one affirmation into your smartphone each morning as a reminder to use it three to five times daily. You can download a printable copy of these affirmations at the website for this book: http://www.newharbinger.com/40705.

Monday: *I bring awareness to my triggers, and they do not surprise me.*

Tuesday: *I value my recovery, and I choose to avoid my avoidable triggers.*

Wednesday: *I have many ways of coping with triggers.*

Thursday: *Triggers are part of recovery, and I am prepared to deal with them.*

Friday: *I recognize my triggers and use my coping kit to center myself.*

Saturday: *I find healthy ways of engaging with my feelings.*

Sunday: *In recovery, I discover new people, places, and things.*

24

Coping with Cravings

The art of being wise is knowing what to overlook.

—**William James**

Oh, cravings. You can't talk about addiction without talking about cravings. And you can't have a healthy recovery without learning how to deal with them. Staying strong and happy beyond addiction means avoiding relapse, and avoiding relapse means moving through cravings when they come, because they *will* come. It's only natural. Cravings can be experienced very intensely in early recovery. They can come even after years of happy recovery. And it's good to be prepared!

The most important thing to know is that cravings are cravings, not *commands*. Cravings are simply urges. There is no reason you have to obey them. The truth is that you move through urges all day long. You may have an urge to sleep through your alarm, to buy a car you can't afford, or to curse at your boss. We are guessing you usually get up for work, save up before buying the car, and don't give your boss an earful. You also probably don't make a face when you don't like your mother-in-law's meatloaf or scratch yourself in certain places in public (even if you're really, really itchy). You notice these urges. You know acting on them wouldn't be a good idea. You move on.

That gives you some very useful information. It means you are stronger and more resilient in the face of cravings than you may think. Various urges you may have don't dictate your behavior. Even when they arise, these urges don't drive you to do things that would harm you. You have the power of choice in the face of your addiction cravings, too.

A craving is like an itch. It may be mild, like a tickle in your nose, or it may be intense, like poison ivy all over your legs. Either way, you have a *choice* about how to respond to the sensation: the desire to scratch the poison ivy may be strong, but it's still just a desire. You don't have to act on it. In fact, if you knew that scratching could lead to scarring on your legs, you would probably find other ways besides scratching to cope with that itchy feeling. Maybe you would distract yourself with something fun, ask a friend to keep you company (someone who would support your plan *not to scratch*), or soothe yourself with some music or a nice, warm bath. You can think of addiction cravings the same way.

Yes, we know that the craving to engage in your addiction can feel stronger than any itch. But in recovery, you are stronger than any craving! You have choices about how you handle a craving. Remember, cravings are not commands!

Exercise: Making a Plan for Cravings

Complete this writing exercise in your journal. If you have a counselor or a therapist, you might ask for help with this, but it's okay to do it on your own, too.

Find a quiet place, without distraction, and gift yourself about thirty minutes to write in your journal. Begin by breathing slowly and deeply, bringing your full attention to this moment. Notice the way your body feels in your chair; notice how the chair holds you and supports you through this exercise. Set an intention that whatever you need to know will be revealed to you.

Now, label the top of one page *healthy distractions*. Label the top of the next page *helpful people*. Label the top of the next page *self-soothing*. Label the top of the next page *I can*.

Under *healthy distractions*, list as many activities or tasks as you can think of that will engage your mind and body and help you to wait out a craving. All of these activities should be done mindfully (not absent-mindedly while you obsess about your craving) and should be unlikely to trigger further cravings. Going for a walk is a great idea, for example, but not if you walk by your old liquor store! Some other good examples might include taking a hot shower, walking around the mall, playing guitar, exercising, watching a funny movie, organizing your closet, going for a drive, reading a magazine, cooking, playing with your dog, having a dance party in your living room…

Under *helpful people,* list as many people as you can think of whom you can call when you are experiencing a craving. After each name, write "share" if you plan to tell that person about your craving, "ask" if you think it would be more helpful to ask that person about his or her day (and distract yourself by supporting someone else), or "chat" if you would just like to talk without sharing about your craving. We know whom you may want to call could vary from moment to moment, and this list is not set in stone.

For *self-soothing,* list as many activities as you can think of that will soothe and relax you. Some examples may include gently stroking your arms, shoulders, or cheeks, taking a hot bath, doing yoga or stretching, looking at pictures of the ocean or other natural spaces, holding a blanket or a stuffed animal, daydreaming about something wonderful, petting your dog or cat…

For *I can,* list as many positive coping statements as you can think of. Some examples may include

- *I have moved through cravings before and I can do it again.*

- *My craving is only temporary.*

- *I have worked hard to recover, and cravings won't trick me into relapse.*

- *I am proud of my recovery from addiction.*

- *I can handle cravings and urges.*

- *I can use my self-soothing methods as I wait out this craving.*

- *I can use healthy distraction as I wait out this craving.*

- *I can reach out to someone as I wait out this craving.*

Return to these pages often, whether your craving is big or small. The more you practice moving through your cravings in these ways, the stronger you will feel!

Affirmations for Coping with Cravings

We recommend you say these affirmations out loud throughout the day to connect with your intention of a mindful recovery. We also recommend you type one affirmation into your smartphone each morning as a reminder to use it three to five times daily. You can download a printable copy of these affirmations at the website for this book: http://www.newharbinger.com/40705.

Monday: *Cravings are a natural part of my recovery, and I move through them naturally.*

Tuesday: *I know I can tolerate cravings just like any other urge.*

Wednesday: *I embrace my recovery; relapse does not appeal to me.*

Thursday: *I can and will move through my urges to use.*

Friday: *Cravings are not commands.*

Saturday: *I make choices in my recovery, and I choose to move through cravings.*

Sunday: *All cravings are temporary.*

25

Reconnecting to Cues

Remember, you cannot abandon what you do not know.
To go beyond yourself, you must know yourself.

—Nisargadatta Maharaj

It is so easy to lose yourself when you are addicted. As the addictive behavior moved from enjoyable to problematic to compulsive, it took up more and more space. Your addiction began to crowd out the other parts of you. Recovery from addiction is about more than casting the addiction out of your life. It is about taking back the things your addiction stole from you. As you try each of the mindfulness exercises in this book, you are reclaiming pieces of yourself.

An important place to start is by reclaiming the connection to your bodily and emotional *cues*, or signals, that you may have lost in your addiction. In an addiction, you can lose touch with your basic feelings so much so that every feeling begins to be labeled as a craving (Flores 2004). Experiencing every sensation as a craving is a risk for relapse. It also makes it very hard to practice healthy self-care: how can you care for yourself if you don't know what you need?

Think of it like this. If you brought me an ice cream sundae when I said I was hungry, I would be pretty excited. But if you brought me an ice cream sundae when I told you I had a stomachache, I would think, *You are not listening to me*, or maybe I would think, *You don't care about what I need*. Either way, the next time I had a stomachache (or any other problem), I would hesitate to tell you about it. The same thing happens between you and your body. If you keep sending your body the message that you don't understand or respect its cues, it is going to hold back from communicating with you. Your body's messages will get quieter and harder to decipher. That's not what you want. It is not the kind of beautiful connection to yourself that healthy recovery deserves.

Send your body the message that you are listening. Let it know that you will respond to its needs with loving care. Reconnect to your cues by learning to PAUSE: *pause, ask, understand*, exercise *self-care*, and *engage*.

Exercise: Practicing PAUSE to Reconnect

Practice this exercise below at least once a day for the next week. You don't need to be in a quiet or isolated place for this meditation, because you want to learn to hear and respond to your cues even under stress or in a crowd. Move through the steps using a journal to explore the process further. Devote yourself to this practice and see what you learn.

P: Pause. This is your starting place, and probably the most important part. You need to find your place of calm and clarity before you can act from it. Give yourself a moment. There is always enough time to take one breath. Maybe you will even gift yourself with another, and another.

A: Ask. By pausing, you have sent yourself the message that you are ready to listen. Now ask yourself what you are feeling. *Am I hungry?* Turn your attention to your stomach and any sensations there. *Am I tired?* Take some time to think about how you know when you are tired. Some people experience this as a desire to itch or rub their eyes; sometimes the head feels heavy; some people tend to yawn or sigh. *Am I experiencing an emotion, such as anger, fear, hurt, or embarrassment?* Do your best to identify the feeling. We know this can be tough. Look back at chapters 6 and 7 for more help with this. *Am I getting enough support?* Be humble enough to know when going it alone just isn't working. Everyone needs help from others, especially in recovery.

U: Understand. Acknowledge to yourself that you have gotten the message. Tell yourself that you understand there is something to be addressed here, and you have an idea about what it is, just as you would assure a friend that you were listening by saying, "I hear you and I get it." Also understand that if you guess wrong—if you decide you are angry when really hunger is the problem—it's truly okay. This is a learning process. Simply taking the time to pay attention in this way means you are on the right track.

S: Self-care. Once you have decided what cues you are experiencing, decide how to take care of yourself. What do you need in this moment? If you are hungry, what will nourish you? If you are tired, do you need to sleep or would some fresh air perk you up? An act of self-care shouldn't set you up to feel even worse afterward. (That's a good way to tell the difference between healthy self-care and potentially harmful self-indulgence). If you are experiencing emotions, how will you greet them and allow them to pass gracefully? If you need more support, how can you reach out and get it?

E: Engage. Practice your self-care! Give yourself what you need. Don't hesitate. Know deep in your core, in that place where wisdom is living, that you deserve to be taken care of. You are not neglecting your body's cues anymore; you are not ignoring your feelings. You are listening with great mindful awareness, and you are now responding from a place of love and care.

Affirmations for Reconnecting to Your Cues

We recommend you say these affirmations out loud throughout the day to connect with your intention of a mindful recovery. We also recommend you type one affirmation into your smartphone each morning as a reminder to use it three to five times daily. You can download a printable copy of these affirmations at the website for this book: http://www.newharbinger.com/40705.

Monday: *I make a commitment to practice PAUSE each day; I am committed to my healthy recovery.*

Tuesday: *I turn my attention inward and discover what I need.*

Wednesday: *Today I will listen to my body and my spirit.*

Thursday: *I am on a journey of understanding my wants and needs.*

Friday: *I know how to nourish myself.*

Saturday: *Self-care is an important and powerful part of my day.*

Sunday: *I choose to listen to myself and take care of my needs. I choose my own well-being.*

26

Urge Surfing

*The only person you are destined to become
is the person you decide to be.*

—Ralph Waldo Emerson

You don't have to live in Southern California to surf the waves! You don't have to pack up and search the best surfing spots in Australia, Costa Rica, or Hawaii (as nice as that sounds). You don't even have to travel at all. You can surf anywhere and anytime with a little imagination and a little bit of curiosity. Let's look at how this works. Grab your imaginary surfboard.

The late Dr. Alan Marlatt coined the term *urge surfing* when he and his team developed mindfulness-based relapse prevention to help people struggling with strong emotions that lead to addictive behaviors be less reactive to urges (Bowen, Chawla, and Marlatt 2010). Surfing your urge allows you to emotionally separate from the experience of the urge. This concept has been widely used to teach people in recovery how to have a different type of relationship with their urges to use drugs, drink alcohol, or engage in risky and destructive behaviors.

Everyone knows that in recovery, urges and cravings will come unannounced. Urges will show up whether they have been invited or not. But you don't have to be tossed around or pulled under by the force of a craving. Instead of giving in to the urge to use, learn to surf!

Exercise 1: Surfing the Urge

Start by practicing this exercise when you have an urge that is mild to moderate, somewhere between 1 and 5 on a scale of 1 to 10. It may be a craving for your addictive behavior or the urge to do something else that does not align with your goals and values. Acknowledge that you are experiencing an urge. Find a private place to sit quietly for five to ten minutes. Close your eyes. Breathe deeply. Notice the urge.

Now visualize this urge as an ocean wave. Notice how the wave builds, peaks, moves downward, and then smooths out again, finally landing calmly at the shore. Cravings move this same way, intensifying and then passing: cravings are *always temporary*. You are the surfer, riding the urge as it begins to swell. Notice yourself on the wave at its peak, and then picture surfing the wave as it starts to drop down back into the ocean. The wave of craving has passed, and you rode it out safely. Take a deep breath as you paddle to shore.

You are now the observer of the urge. All you need is the ability to slow down a bit. The urge will not last forever. The urge is a temporary visitor. It will move on like the waves do.

Audio for the next meditation exercise is available at http://www .newharbinger.com/40705.

Exercise 2: Getting More Mindful with Urges

Living a mindful life means approaching your experiences—all your experiences—with awareness, presence, and curiosity. We welcome you to take this same approach with your urges. Use the following exercise to interact with your urges in a new, mindful way.

Begin by sitting comfortably in a chair. For this exercise, it is not necessary to plant your feet on the floor the way you often do during meditation. You may cross your legs or arms in any position that feels comfortable to you. Set a timer for five minutes so that you don't feel the need to watch the clock. Close your eyes; allow your attention to move inward. Now set the intention to remain still, completely still, for these five minutes.

As you sit quietly, notice your urges. For example, although you chose the position that was most comfortable to you, you may find that as the moment has changed, so has your level of comfort. You may notice an urge to shift in your seat. You may notice the desire to cross or uncross your legs. Perhaps there is an itch you would like to scratch. Imagine that your attuned attention is a flashlight in the dark. Turn the light on each urge and explore it.

Let these questions guide your experience:

• Does each urge seem to intensify over time, or does it fade?

• Do some urges seem to persist? Do some urges seem to come and go?

• How does the mind respond to the urge? Does it begin to throw out judgments such as *I want to move my leg, I have to scratch my nose,* or *How much longer until I'm done here?* If the mind is making these negative judgments, how does the body respond? What happens to the intensity of the urge?

• What happens to the intensity of an urge when you turn your flashlight elsewhere instead?

After your meditation, reflect on the experience. If you gave in to an urge, how did it feel? How did it feel in the moment versus several moments later? Were you able to recommit to your intention, or did you find yourself wanting to abandon the exercise altogether?

How did you cope with urges as they arose? For all the urges you did not give in to, how did you move through that space without acting on them?

Each time you practice this exercise, you are likely to experience it differently. Over time, the more you practice urge surfing and using mindfulness to notice but not act on your urges, the better you will get.

Affirmations for Urge Surfing

We recommend you say these affirmations out loud throughout the day to connect with your intention of a mindful recovery. We also recommend you type one affirmation into your smartphone each morning as a reminder to use it three to five times daily. You can download a printable copy of these affirmations at the website for this book: http://www.newharbinger.com/40705.

Monday: *Urges are a normal part of life; I notice my urges without reacting to them.*

Tuesday: *I feel confident when I ride the wave of my urges.*

Wednesday: *Today I am aware of urges and watch them pass through my mind.*

Thursday: *I remain curious about my ability to observe difficult emotions.*

Friday: *Practicing nonjudgment when urges arise is part of my healthy recovery.*

Saturday: *Today I will imagine I am a surfer riding the wave of my urges.*

Sunday: *My recovery includes kind moments of noticing my urges.*

Mindfulness Skills and Stress Relief

27

Changing Your Perspective on Stress

There is no perfection, only life.

—Milan Kundera

Charlie says, "At some point, I started noticing that whatever I told myself I couldn't handle happening would definitely happen. If I said to myself, *I'll never make it through that interview tomorrow without a good night's sleep*, something crazy would happen, like our fire alarm going off at 2:00 a.m. In the old days, I would have thought I was cursed. I would have used it as an excuse to use, like *The whole world is against me. I might as well get high.* But this time, I decided I'm supposed to be learning something from this stuff. I started realizing I can handle that crappy night's sleep or whatever else I was worrying about. Life has been giving me these opportunities to figure out that I am strong."

Life happens. It happens even when you are simply too busy for any more of it to be happening. And the hard stuff seems to happen all the darn time. You cannot change that fact. But you can make choices about how you respond to what happens in your life. You don't have to feel stressed out all the time.

You see, the truth is that stress does not happen just because life gets hard. Stress happens when life gets hard and *you believe you cannot handle it.*

A lot of people are fooled into thinking that they won't be able to handle life as it comes. They look at the task in front of them and think, *This is too much for me.* Addiction makes life a lot harder, and it limits your ability to see your own strength. Your addiction was limiting you for a long time. Maybe your addiction tried to trick you into feeling weak. In your mindful recovery, you have the chance to find your strength. You get to discover what you are really capable of, to see how the hard stuff helps you grow. When life gets tough, see how you can rise to the challenge. See that you indeed can handle what comes your way.

Exercise: Changing Your Perspective on Stress

For this exercise, you will be taking a mindful walk. Walking in a place that includes nature (trees or plants, water, clear views of the sky) would be preferable, but you can engage in this experience in any place you choose. The world is changing all the time, and so are you. Even if you have been in this place before, you have never been in this place as it is now. And you have never been in this place as the person you are in this moment. It makes sense, then, to explore your surroundings with curiosity.

Take a short walk, just about ten to fifteen minutes. Walk slowly, engaging each of your five senses as you explore what you encounter.

Pay attention to colors and shapes. Notice the way the light is falling in this place. Are there shadows or shade? Notice what happens to the color of an object when it is in the light or in the shade.

Bring your attention to the sounds in this environment. What do you hear? Does each sound seem close or distant? Notice the sounds you make as you move through this space.

As you continue your walk, attend to your sense of smell. What scents are in the air here? If you come across plants of any kind, lean in and engage with their smell.

When you come across an interesting object, pick it up and hold it or reach out and touch it (as long as this is safe). Notice its edges and any markings on its surface. Notice its weight and texture.

You may not feel comfortable tasting what is around you (and shouldn't if it isn't safe), but take a moment to bring your attention to what's happening inside your mouth as you explore where you are. Notice the placement of your tongue against the hard palate, the tip of the tongue against your teeth and lips. Take a sip of water if you brought a bottle with you. Feel the refreshing swirl of cool water inside your mouth as you swallow.

Pay attention to the temperature and how your body feels in the air around you. Notice the sensations of your body as you walk.

When you arrive home, sit with your journal and reflect on this experience. How did being truly present and curious about your environment change the way you see things? Notice if you feel less stressed. Keep in mind that simple experiences can change your relationship with stress.

Affirmations for Changing Your Perspective on Stress

We recommend you say these affirmations out loud throughout the day to connect with your intention of a mindful recovery. We also recommend you type one affirmation into your smartphone each morning as a reminder to use it three to five times daily. You can download a printable copy of these affirmations at the website for this book: http://www .newharbinger.com/40705.

Monday: *I can handle the things that seem hard.*

Tuesday: *I allow myself to see that I am strong.*

Wednesday: *I can handle whatever comes my way.*

Thursday: *I am stronger than I knew.*

Friday: *My challenges do not bring me down; I rise above them.*

Saturday: *My obstacles are opportunities.*

Sunday: *Life gives me the chance to see what I am capable of.*

28

Progressive Muscle Relaxation

Body awareness is the place where transformation happens.

—Ann Weiser Cornell

Even though Ethan was nearing one year of sobriety, he still felt tense, anxious, and irritable most days. He felt keyed up at work, was frustrated with his friends, and still had trouble falling asleep at night. He thought that by now things would be fixed. He thought he would be able to manage the day-to-day stressors better. In fact, it sometimes felt like the tension was taking over, and sometimes he even felt like using again just to get some relief. You might be in the same boat as Ethan. You've heard there are lots of ways to manage stress, but if stress is so manageable, how come you feel tense all the time? Is there something missing from your life that can help decrease tension on a regular basis?

Learning how to relax could be one of the most important things you do to keep your recovery on track. We are going to review a specific technique called *progressive muscle relaxation* with you. This stress management technique has been around a long time. It was originally developed by Dr. Edmund Jacobson (1978) when he discovered a link between muscle tension and disorders of the mind and body (Davis, Eshelman, and McKay 2008). The basic idea behind this technique is that an anxious mind can't exist in a relaxed body, and deeply relaxing your body makes it very hard for your mind to stay stressed.

Progressive muscle relaxation has been used in many detox and recovery treatment programs to help people cope with the physical and emotional stress of recovery from addiction. It is especially useful for people in recovery who are returning to their busy everyday lives. Maybe like Ethan you turned to your addiction partly because you were trying to decrease tension. Progressive muscle relaxation is one way to manage that tension without returning to substances. Ethan was excited to try this technique to help him decrease tension and reengage with a healthy recovery.

Progressive muscle relaxation focuses on tensing and then releasing each of your muscle groups. As you do this, you experience the difference between when you feel tense and when you feel relaxed. Doing this exercise will make you more aware of your physical world, just as you have become more aware of your thoughts and emotions.

Exercise: Using Progressive Muscle Relaxation

Find a quiet place. It could be in your office with the door closed, at home in the evening before bed, or some other place that gives you peace. You can do this exercise seated on a chair or lying down on your back. Generally, lying down is preferred, but it's not always practical. Progressive muscle relaxation is also helpful if you are having trouble falling asleep.

Give yourself about fifteen to twenty uninterrupted minutes to complete this exercise. We will go through the whole body, one muscle group at a time. You can always choose just a few muscle groups to start with. Note: Consult your doctor or health professional if you have questions about progressive muscle relaxation prior to starting the exercise.

Take your shoes off here, and if you wear glasses, remove them for this exercise. Begin by starting with your *hands*. Inhale and clench your hands tightly for five seconds, and then exhale and relax completely and let your hands go for twenty seconds. Then move up to your *wrists* and *forearms*: extend them and bend your hands back at the wrist, hold for five seconds, and release for twenty seconds. Next go to your *biceps* and *upper arms*: squeeze your hands into fists, bend your arms at the elbow and flex your biceps for five seconds, and then relax your arms for twenty seconds. Shrug your *shoulders* up to your ears for five seconds; then release your shoulders for twenty seconds. Crinkle your *forehead* into a frown and hold it for five seconds; then relax your forehead for twenty seconds. Close your *eyes* tightly (remove contact lenses before you start this exercise) for five seconds; then relax your eyes and around your nose for twenty seconds. For your *cheeks* and *jaw,* make a wide smile and hold it for five seconds; then relax your cheeks and jaw for twenty seconds. Pay special attention to your *neck:* touch your chin to your chest, hold for five seconds, and then release your neck back to upright for twenty seconds. Focus on your *chest* next: take a deep breath and hold it for five to ten seconds; then exhale for twenty seconds. When you are ready, suck your *stomach* in tight for five seconds; then release it for twenty seconds. Next move to your *hips* and *buttocks:* tighten your buttocks, and then relax into the chair or floor for twenty seconds. Tighten your *thighs* and hold for five seconds; then release your thighs for twenty seconds. Finally, focus on your *lower legs;* point your toes upward toward your face; then point your toes away and curl your toes for five seconds, and then relax your legs and toes for twenty seconds.

Once you have tensed and relaxed all muscle groups, take a beautiful in-breath and out-breath. Again, inhale and exhale. Count backwards from five to one to bring yourself back to the present moment. Notice how you are feeling. Take a mini-inventory of your body. Can you feel the difference between your body with tension and your body when it relaxes? You now can offer your body brief periods of relaxation in support of your recovery. Progressive muscle relaxation is another tool to add to your stress relief toolbox.

Affirmations for Stress Relief

We recommend you say these affirmations out loud throughout the day to connect with your intention of a mindful recovery. We also recommend you type one affirmation into your smartphone each morning as a reminder to use it three to five times daily. You can download a printable copy of these affirmations at the website for this book: http://www.newharbinger.com/40705.

Monday: *Today I give myself fifteen minutes to practice progressive muscle relaxation.*

Tuesday: *Relaxation skills take practice. I allow the time to practice for my recovery.*

Wednesday: *I notice when I am carrying tension and allow myself to let it go.*

Thursday: *My recovery has room for a short relaxation technique today.*

Friday: *Returning my attention to my physical body improves my wellness.*

Saturday: *My body needs time to relax today.*

Sunday: *Stress relief is an important part of my recovery.*

29

Removing Unnecessary Stress

*No amount of anxiety makes any difference
to anything that is going to happen.*

—Alan Watts

Stress. In this day and age, it is practically a way of life. For some of us, it seems to sneak into almost every moment: at work, at home, even waking us up in the night. Some of your stress is inevitable, and accepting that fact will be part of your healthy recovery. But there are also a whole host of stressors that you may actually be choosing for yourself. Some stress is not mandatory: this is *unnecessary stress*. Here are a few common types of unnecessary stressors.

Social Media

For some people, social media is a wonderful way to connect with others, to share joys and challenges, and to stay in touch. For many others, it is a black hole, an alternate reality in which everyone you know seems to be taking awesome vacations, raising perfect children, and attending fabulous events. Everything they do is worthy of a photo op; even their food looks better than yours. Our clients often have trouble avoiding their most painful and challenging stressors when they are online: ex-boyfriends or ex-girlfriends, for example, or friendships that have ended badly. Losing a relationship is incredibly hard. Not being able to escape the details of that person's life is devastating, even crazy making.

If any of this is happening to you, it is time to make some choices. The truth is, you won't die without social media. Life, even your social life, will go on without it. You might decide to take a break from social media to see how it feels. You might decide to give it up completely. Or you might decide to make some very specific decisions about how to use the sites you visit and whom you allow into this social world with you. Whatever you choose to do about it, acknowledge for yourself if social media is stressing you out, and realize that this stress is truly optional.

The News

Watching the news can be another cause of stress. While it may be important to keep yourself informed, if it doesn't result in positive action and it does cause chronic stress, it may be time to reevaluate. For some of our clients, the news is doing nothing for them but worsening their depression, increasing their anxiety, and leading to relapse. For these clients, we recommend a TV diet. Just like cutting back on foods that leave you feeling junky, cutting out or cutting back on the TV that stresses you out can really help you. Maybe you will decide that watching only the world news or only the local news or limiting your news to once a week results in less stress. It's up to you!

Living Beyond Your Means

Spending more than you earn puts you on the fast track to stress. It's easy to feel like you are living in quicksand when you continuously put yourself in debt. You do have other options. Create a budget and be realistic about the difference between wants and needs. If your existing debt is stressing you out, get some help. There are many organizations set up to support you in managing and moving through debt. You can relieve this stress by being genuinely honest with yourself about the lifestyle you can actually afford, and then working on accepting this.

Being an Overachiever

While there is nothing inherently wrong with working hard, achieving, or striving, being a perfectionist can lead to stress. If you are finding yourself stressed out all the time, you may decide you are sacrificing too much by living this way. If nothing ever seems like enough, if there is always another plateau you must reach (where, you are sure, happiness must be waiting for you), you are in a trap. Time to find your way out. Let good enough be good enough. Find your joy today, in this moment. It doesn't reside anywhere else.

In the end, you will have to decide for yourself whether these stressors are ones you want to keep. You have to decide if they are worth it. Sometimes the pleasure outweighs the pain. If it is your choice to keep these unnecessary stressors in your life, own them. Know that these things are stressing you out, and realize that you are consciously choosing this stress because it is worth it to you. But if the stress doesn't really feel worthwhile, remember that these stressors are unnecessary; they are voluntary. You really can let them go!

Exercise: Meditation for Removing Unnecessary Stress

Sit quietly in a comfortable place without distractions. Begin by focusing on your breath, making sure it becomes slow, deep, and soothing. Take as long as you need to become centered and peaceful.

Now that you are present in this moment, take this time to ask for some clarity. You are seeking wisdom. Pose the question gently, and welcome the answers that come. Ask yourself, What are my stressors?

This is a meditation for self-exploration. You are not feeling your stress at this moment. It is not arising in the body. You are observing it. You are only witnessing it. If it does show up in the body, notice this and let it move outward, flowing gently away from you in any direction you choose.

As a stressor pops into the mind, let your intuition tell you whether it is time to release it. If something is telling you that this is unnecessary stress, listen. Honor that feeling. You don't need to make any firm decisions. You don't need to commit. Today you are seeking understanding. Visualize the stressor that you want to release as a bubble floating far away from you until it disappears. See how that feels. You may practice this for as long as you like. Write in your journal about this experience. Thank your inner wisdom for being available to you today.

Affirmations for Removing Unnecessary Stress

We recommend you say these affirmations out loud throughout the day to connect with your intention of a mindful recovery. We also recommend you type one affirmation into your smartphone each morning as a reminder to use it three to five times daily. You can download a printable copy of these affirmations at the website for this book: http://www.newharbinger.com/40705.

Monday:	*I take an honest look at my stressors and see which ones I can let go.*
Tuesday:	*I can accept my inevitable stress.*
Wednesday:	*If my stressor is worthwhile, I will take the good with the bad.*
Thursday:	*I am willing to release my unnecessary stress.*
Friday:	*I know there are ways I can decrease my stress. I see where I can let stressors fall away from my life.*
Saturday:	*I do not hold on to any stressor that creates more pain than pleasure.*
Sunday:	*I choose peace and contentment over stress.*

30

Practicing Acceptance

Whatever the present moment contains, accept it as if you had chosen it. Always work with it, not against it.

—Eckhart Tolle

A few months ago, I (Julie) had a flea infestation. At first it was just an itchy dog; then we started to see them, once or twice a day, here or there. Before long, fleas were in the carpets, in our bed, and, worst of all, bouncing off my two-year-old. Nine months pregnant, I was in a panic. We had to get this under control before the baby came! We launched a full-scale attack on the critters: organic powders, expensive flea meds for the dog, and a complete debugging by the exterminator. But our first night home from the hospital, as I unswaddled my newborn, a flea jumped out from his blanket.

Had you told me to be patient at that moment, I hesitate to tell you what I would have said in response. But the fact is, I had to accept this. See, fleas have a life cycle. The eggs had to hatch and die off, and until that happened, we were going to see a few fleas. No matter how hard we tried to control the situation, we were going to have to wait.

In your life, and especially in early recovery, you may have a type of infestation of your very own to deal with. Problems that developed when you were in your addiction may seem to be bouncing all around you. Your relationships, work life, finances, and health may all be in sorry shape. Not to mention the cravings, the roller coaster of emotions, and life situations that you are learning to cope with in recovery. It is easy to feel overwhelmed. Getting to a place where life runs more smoothly is going to take some work. It sure won't happen as fast as you would like. What's great is that you don't have to sit around waiting for life to smooth out. You can tolerate your experiences as they are right now. It is time to practice *acceptance*.

Acceptance is a way of acknowledging what is. You are no longer raging or pushing against reality. You are not responding to what happens in your life with *That's not fair, I can't stand this,* or *It shouldn't be this way.* You breathe deeply and understand that *It is what it is.*

Acceptance doesn't mean that you think it's okay or that you like the way it is. You accept your life as it is in this moment because resisting it is pointless. And infuriating. And exhausting. Resistance takes what is uncomfortable or painful and turns it into all-out suffering. By contrast, practicing acceptance keeps the difficult stuff only as difficult as it is. It allows your challenges to be as they are instead of intensifying them. When you practice acceptance, you send a deep and powerful message to yourself that you can tolerate whatever comes. Over time, practicing acceptance will allow you to feel truly safe and secure. You know that even in the hard, painful moments, you will be okay.

We call it *practicing* acceptance because acceptance really does require practice. Don't expect yourself to be perfect at this or at any of the skills you are learning! Give yourself some patience and set an intention to grow in this area.

Exercise: Practicing Acceptance

Set aside about twenty minutes to do this exercise. You can do this alone, or you can include loved ones who understand and support what you are trying to do. You will need ten note cards and some colored markers.

On each note card, write the phrase "It is what it is." Breathe deeply and hold the phrase gently in your mind each time that you write it. If you feel comfortable, say the words out loud.

Now choose the places in your world that you will most benefit from remembering to practice acceptance. Maybe you will tape a note card next to your bed, on your bathroom mirror, or on the fridge. Maybe you will put one in your gym bag or purse or on the dashboard of your car or even on your computer at work.

Life will give you plenty of opportunities to practice acceptance each and every day. Use your note cards as reminders to respond to your challenges with gentle, patient acceptance. Breathe deeply and notice the changes this newfound acceptance brings to your life in recovery.

Affirmations for Practicing Acceptance

We recommend you say these affirmations out loud throughout the day to connect with your intention of a mindful recovery. We also recommend you type one affirmation into your smartphone each morning as a reminder to use it three to five times daily. You can download a printable copy of these affirmations at the website for this book: http://www.newharbinger.com/40705.

Monday: *It is what it is.*

Tuesday: *Today I accept what is.*

Wednesday: *I practice acceptance for a healthy recovery.*

Thursday: *I can tolerate the things I don't like.*

Friday: *Resistance to what is will only exhaust me. I choose to be healthy.*

Saturday: *I am learning to accept what comes my way.*

Sunday: *I greet my challenges with patient acceptance.*

31

Decluttering Your Space

Get rid of clutter and you may just find it was blocking
the door you've been looking for.

—Katrina Mayer

If just the idea of decluttering gives you heart palpitations and cold sweats, then stop right here. Close the book. It's not the right time to try this exercise. If you are worried that we are going to ask you to throw away all your stuff, don't worry. Your decisions will always be up to you. If even the thought of decluttering your space feels like too much, it's okay. You have permission to revisit this later or never.

However, if you had a sneaking suspicion that your clutter and messiness are somehow connected to your recovery, but you don't know how, then take a deep breath. That's good. Take another deep breath. This is one of those gifts that you really did not ask for, but it's right in front of you anyway. We want the idea of decluttering your space to be another curiosity for you. Be gentle with yourself here. There are a lot of emotions tied up in things, especially old things. On the one hand, some of your things may hold memories of times you were active in your addiction. Maybe you kept too many things to protect yourself without even knowing it. You may be buried in *I may need this one day* stuff. Or *this was a gift from my old boyfriend* stuff. Or *this was expensive, I can't get rid of it* stuff. The natural reaction is to ignore the stuff, say you will deal with it later, or hide it away in a closet or drawer.

On the other hand, some of your things may represent times when you were doing well and connected with others. But sometimes these items that bring you happiness are lost somewhere in the mess.

The job here is to begin the process of figuring out what characterizes the person you are now. An honest and respectful look at yourself and your space is what you are up to now. You get to connect with the person who is more in touch with thoughts and feelings and less reactive to life's inevitable ups and downs. As Elbert Hubbard once wrote, "The sculptor produces the beautiful statue by chipping away such parts of the marble block as are not needed—it is a process of elimination." The same is true when decluttering your space. You will be chipping away at those objects that are no longer needed, as you reconnect with the healthy and wise parts of yourself. You will be simplifying your space to make room to feel better and become more in tune with calm feelings. Cleaning up not only creates a nicer space for you but also has a positive effect on your mind and emotions.

Exercise: Decluttering Your Space

You are ready to get started on the delightful experience of decluttering. Use the acronym SPACE to remind you of a few skills to incorporate as you move through decluttering and cleaning up.

S: Sit still. Before you take on the task of decluttering, sit still in meditation. Take a moment to give thanks for everything that has come into your life. Acknowledge you will be letting some things go to reconnect with who you are now. Also give thanks for your space, your home. This space is your sanctuary and the space in which you have spent most of your time. Take three deep breaths.

P: Pleasant experience. Link the actions of decluttering and cleaning up with one or more enjoyable experiences. For example, put on your favorite music, light a wonderfully scented candle, turn on your diffuser with calming essential oils, enjoy a cup of flavorful tea, or even invite a good friend over to share in the experience. Allow your friend to give you candid feedback. Be open and curious. Start with one area of your home, perhaps the kitchen. Start with opening the fridge and looking to see what you can throw away. Then clean the inside of the fridge. Well done. Move on to another area of your space.

A: Ask yourself. With every item that you touch, ask yourself, *Does this item enhance my recovery?* How do you feel when you hold the item? How are you feeling as you release the item? Do you feel refreshed, sad, confused, or surprisingly free? Messy, dirty, disorganized spaces may be mirrored in your mind without you even realizing it. Notice all feelings you have, without judgment, as your space begins to change. Move on to the next item.

C: Charity. Giving to others is an important part of your recovery. Make three boxes. The donate box, the throwaway box, and the friend/family box. Donate items that are in good condition to your favorite local charity. Throw away items that are broken, torn, or just plain no good to anyone. Decide which items you would like to offer to a friend or family member who might enjoy them. Set time aside within this week to take the boxes to charity and to your friends or family members. Continue to move through each of your spaces with this same plan.

E: Embrace your new space. Some people feel like they are in a whole new space as they release items. Decluttering changes the energy of your space. You, too, may feel less distracted and more relaxed and focused. Give your space room to take care of you, and give your mind room to expand. After a long day, your home will greet you with open arms and a warm smile. Welcome home.

Affirmations for Decluttering Your Space

We recommend you say these affirmations out loud throughout the day to connect with your intention of a mindful recovery. We also recommend you type one affirmation into your smartphone each morning as a reminder to use it three to five times daily. You can download a printable copy of these affirmations at the website for this book: http://www.newharbinger.com/40705.

Monday: *I make room for my thoughts and feelings by letting go of items I no longer need.*

Tuesday: *My intention is to live in a calm and peaceful home.*

Wednesday: *Today I focus on one goal at a time without worrying about the outcome.*

Thursday: *My home is a sanctuary where I can rest and restore myself.*

Friday: *I accept exactly where I am and allow my space to be part of my recovery journey.*

Saturday: *The things around me represent my healthy recovery.*

Sunday: *Even small changes in my space help me to feel restored.*

SECTION 7

Cultivating Relationships

32

Creating a Support System
(and Using It)

Sometimes the shortest distance between two points
is a winding path walked arm in arm.

—Robert Brault

Hope. It was one thing that was missing from Derrick's recovery. He was doing the things he was supposed to do from day to day, but he felt lost, alone, and increasingly negative. Derrick went to a recovery aftercare group but never participated. He usually left the group early so he would not have to talk to anyone. A few group members reached out to him but with no luck. His brother was the only one in his family who knew he had stopped using drugs. He didn't speak to anyone else. Derrick, in a moment of reflection, asked himself: *How can I feel hopeful again?*

People who have a strong support system have a higher chance of sustaining recovery. Think of a support system as your tribe. It's a group of people who care about you, who are there when times get rough and life feels overwhelming. Creating and using a support system has lots of interesting benefits. A healthy support system can improve your mood, your health, your spiritual connections, and even your self-esteem. And if you are feeling disconnected from others, having a support system will help you reconnect. A support system will give you someone to talk to, someone who is open to hearing about what is bothering you, and that person will remind you of your goals for a happy and connected life. Everyone needs support when they feel like relapsing into old thoughts and behaviors. Your support system can be that place to land when you are feeling unsteady in your recovery. It's harder to withdraw from social interactions when you have people in place who know you and whom you can reach out to. Other people in recovery who are part of your support system will know when you may be on the verge of moving in unhealthy directions and will be able to gently bring you back to the here and now. And if you have an emergency, they will be there for you.

You can mindfully create a support system by attending meetings, talking to your family or friends, finding a mental health professional to meet with on a regular basis, or attending your local church or religious organization. Reach out. We want you to be curious about what you need at this stage of your recovery.

Creating your support system is an important step. The next step is to use it! Practice reaching out in your recovery. Pick up the phone, send an e-mail, or ask someone to meet. You may feel awkward or shy, so remember to feel the feelings you have, without judgment. Chances are other people have had similar feelings when interacting with others. Connect with others on a week-to-week basis whether you feel like you need the support or not. Interacting with other supportive people when you are doing well is important too! Others would love to know that you are feeling good and enjoying life. Share your positive experiences and feelings in your recovery. And don't forget to share any resources you have and to pick up resources others may have about things that will nourish your recovery.

Exercise 1: Acknowledging Your Support System

This is a writing exercise. Use your journal or a notepad. Allow yourself ten to fifteen minutes of quiet, uninterrupted time. Make a list of all the people who have been supportive of you in the past, whether the support was financial, emotional, spiritual, at work, or in recovery. Your list could include family, friends, acquaintances, coworkers, church members, Anonymous group members, aftercare members, counselors, doctors, nurses, therapists, nutritionists, mentors, teachers, and even neighbors. Write down anyone who comes to mind who has been kind to you. Once you have this list of supportive people, review it and put a check mark next to anyone who has been above-and-beyond supportive in your recovery. Choose one of these people and write him or her a brief thank-you letter, something like: "I wanted to take this opportunity to thank you for your support and encouragement. It has meant the world to me. I really appreciate you." One way to enhance your support system is to express gratitude. Take a deep breath and enjoy the experience of cherishing and using your support system.

Exercise 2: Making Support a Healthy Habit

For the next week, commit to calling one friend, family member, or recovering acquaintance every day. Send one e-mail, letter, postcard, or message on social media to another person each day. It is up to you how much you share or what you talk about with each person. Get into the habit of reaching out. See how it feels to grow and connect with your support system.

Affirmations for Creating a Support System

We recommend you say these affirmations out loud throughout the day to connect with your intention of a mindful recovery. We also recommend you type one affirmation into your smartphone each morning as a reminder to use it three to five times daily. You can download a printable copy of these affirmations at the website for this book: http://www .newharbinger.com/40705.

Monday: *I know the true meaning of a good support system in my recovery.*

Tuesday: *My well-being depends on my connection to my support system.*

Wednesday: *Today I reach out to at least one person in my support system.*

Thursday: *Building a quality support system is taking care of myself.*

Friday: *I feel hopeful when I think about my support network.*

Saturday: *I offer my support and kindness to one person today.*

Sunday: *I show my gratitude to those who have supported me in my journey.*

33

Relationships That Don't Work

Nothing ever goes away until it has taught us what we need to know.

—Pema Chödrön

Staying in a relationship longer than it is providing mutual support is very common. To know if a relationship is working, you'll need to understand when a relationship is *not* working. This may include relationships with friends, romantic partners, family members, and even sponsors. In recovery, being honest about your relationships is even more challenging. You may have had close relationships with others who used drugs or alcohol, or who engaged in destructive behaviors. And they may still be active in their addiction. It may have been difficult to be truthful in some of your relationships. Or perhaps you did not have an easy way of interacting, feeling too shy, too loud, or too controlling.

Some people will be able to come along with you on your recovery journey; others may not. As you live a recovering life, you will most likely need to reassess your connections with others. We have outlined six ways you may be able to see if your relationship is not working. As we hope you do with all our exercises, be kind to yourself as you explore your thoughts and feelings here.

Focus on one relationship that you believe might not be working to support your recovering life. Put a check mark next to any of these statements that rings true for you.

1. You are in a different place in your life and your recovery, but the other person does not acknowledge it or care.

2. You are making significant changes in your life, and the other person isn't (and/or ridicules you for the changes you have made so far).

3. You and the other person have vastly different goals for the relationship, and sometimes your goals are completely opposite to each other.

4. Your emotions (anger, resentment, fear, disgust) are running hot and seem to be getting stronger in this relationship.

5. You find yourself blaming the other person for just about everything, and the other person blames you just as much.

6. You don't like the person you are becoming in this relationship.

If you checked one, two, or three of these, it's time to have an honest talk with this person about how you are feeling and how you would like the relationship to change. Remember to take responsibility for your part of the tension, and focus on how you want to be part of the solution. If you checked four or more of these, reflect on whether this relationship is meeting your needs and if you are willing to put the work in to improve it. All healthy relationships take energy and commitment. It is up to you to allow time with yourself to understand the signs and make a heartfelt decision about the relationship.

There is an opportunity to reconnect with what you value now, what matters to you. Be honest with yourself and ask, *Is this relationship supporting my vision of myself?* If the answer is yes, continue to move forward, have candid communication, listen, and express yourself. Perhaps this would be a good time to talk to a counselor or therapist about new ways to interact; a relationship counselor may have ideas on how to manage your changing relationship in recovery. And if the answer is no—if this relationship is not supporting your vision of yourself—be kind to yourself and learn how to let go with respect for yourself and the other person.

Spend time figuring out what you need in your relationships and figuring out the person you want to be in your relationships. You may notice yourself feeling calm and surprisingly resilient as you reconnect with your true self. Let each relationship teach you about yourself. You are ready to see what the future has in store for you.

Exercise: Releasing Relationships That Don't Work

This exercise is a visualization. Find a quiet place and allow yourself fifteen to twenty minutes of uninterrupted time. Sit comfortably and close your eyes. Let your shoulders relax, and loosen your jaw. Breathe. First, visualize all the people in your life who are supportive of you and your recovery: friends, family members, spouse, partner, mentor, sponsor, even colleagues who are there for you. Take a few minutes to experience what it feels like to be so supported and loved. Visualize these people showering you with love and encouragement. Everyone is looking at you with kindness and reassurance. Take a deep breath. Inhale through your nose and exhale through your mouth. Take two more breaths like that. Good. Notice the feeling of warmth and compassion flow through you. Wonderful.

Second, visualize that person who is no longer lining up with your idea of yourself. Stay calm and relaxed. Visualize yourself giving that person the same warmth and compassion you are feeling from your loved ones. Accept that the relationship is not working out at this point in your life. Acknowledge that you did your best. In your mind, shower forgiveness over yourself and this person. Inhale and exhale. Let go and be well. Remember, this mindfulness exercise is about enhancing your recovery. And the best way to do this is to practice acceptance and forgiveness, even when relationships do not work out. Slowly open your eyes, move your body, and return to the room. Practice this exercise whenever there is a relationship that is not aligning with your true values.

Affirmations for Letting Go of
Relationships That Don't Work

We recommend you say these affirmations out loud throughout the day to connect with your intention of a mindful recovery. We also recommend you type one affirmation into your smartphone each morning as a reminder to use it three to five times daily. You can download a printable copy of these affirmations at the website for this book: http://www.newharbinger.com/40705.

Monday: *I respect my decision to end a relationship that is not healthy for me.*

Tuesday: *Today I am grateful for the ways my relationships contribute to my recovery.*

Wednesday: *I accept that not all people will come along with me on my journey.*

Thursday: *Forgiving others is a characteristic I honor in myself.*

Friday: *My recovery has room for acceptance of my limitations in relationships.*

Saturday: *I feel support and love from others and offer support and love to others.*

Sunday: *Today I connect with my true values that shine light on my recovery.*

34

Dating and Intimacy

Love must be as much a light as it is a flame.

—Henry David Thoreau

Monique, close to ten months sober, had no idea what intimacy was. She decided to look the word up in the dictionary. When she read the definition out loud: "closely acquainted, familiar, private and personal, made known," she felt sick to her stomach. *Well, that's not going to happen,* she said to herself. The idea of being close to someone, anyone, was a foreign concept. It was like being invited to another planet she was not sure she wanted to visit. Monique's few relationships, if you could call them that, were mostly chaotic and disappointing. Sometimes she felt needy and unwanted. Other times she felt aggressive and fiercely independent. She was afraid to be vulnerable with someone else, and, like most of us, she was afraid of rejection.

If you have had problems with dating and intimacy, we can safely say you are not alone. Recovery brings its fair share of anxiety about how to interact with other people, especially when you are romantically interested. There is a way to mindfully move through this new land of sober dating and connecting. We have put together a few ideas for reflection. You have probably heard that the best intimate relationships are built upon a *friendship connection.* That is why our ideas spell out FRIEND. Take a few moments to see if FRIEND can guide you as you navigate dating and intimacy.

F: Forgive yourself. You have a responsibility to yourself to forgive your conduct in past relationships. Try not to dwell on your past mistakes or to focus on your future expectations. Target your attention to the person you are with right now.

R: Respect the experience. Dating and intimacy in recovery will feel new and different. Give the experience your respect and allow it to unfold without pressure. Respect yourself and the other person with clear communication and kindness.

I: Intention: Create an intention of *how you would like to be* in a relationship rather than a vision of how you want the other person to be. What value will you bring? How will you respond to disconnection and disagreement? How will you respond to a deepening connection? Remind yourself that feeling vulnerable is part of the journey.

E: Empathy. Empathy is your ability to see things from someone else's perspective. When you see things from a perspective other than your own, you learn something new. Now you get to practice empathy as it relates to dating and intimacy.

N: New decisions. You will not be making the same type of decisions about relationships that you made in your addiction. Your decisions will now be serving your best interest and the best interest of your recovery. Trust your instincts. Remember, you can say no to relationships that do not feel right for you.

D: Don't rush. The recommendation in Anonymous groups for people in recovery is to give yourself one year before getting involved in a serious relationship. This isn't to punish you; it's to protect your recovery and your relationships. Getting involved with someone too early in recovery can make it hard to form a healthy relationship. And a problematic relationship or a breakup can trigger relapse. Make sure you have a plan in place to calm your emotions and connect with your well-being.

Learning about dating and intimacy felt like climbing a very tall mountain for Monique. But she was willing to give it a try. This was the first time she heard about FRIEND, and it made sense. For the first time, she felt that she deserved love and affection.

Exercise: Cooking and Connecting Mindfully

This is a mindful-cooking exercise. Cooking mindfully allows you to be aware, without judgment, of all the ingredients that go into your food. It's great practice for being nonjudgmental about dating and intimacy. Even if you feel that cooking isn't your thing, we recommend you breathe, notice what feelings are coming up around cooking, and gently let the feelings go. If you normally rush around and eat on the go, now is a good time to practice slowing down. Mindfully choose a recipe that you would like to cook. Be aware of how you choose the recipe. Next, prepare to go shopping for the ingredients. Take your time picking everything out, and focus on your breathing. Notice the colors, the smells, and the textures of the food. Choose one friend you would like to connect with over a meal. Choose a trusted person. You will be practicing slowing down and connecting without pressure. Decide on the date and time, and invite that person over to help you prepare the food. Begin your preparation. Make the meal with the intention of kindness and connection. Set the table paying special attention to the experience of joining with another person. Be aware of your mood. Serve the food with love. Breathe. Taste the food, notice the flavors, and tap into your well-being and the well-being of this relationship. Use mindful cooking to connect with others in your recovery. Mindful cooking and connecting with a friend are a great rehearsal for connecting with someone you have romantic feelings for. Remember to be kind to yourself as you develop new ways of relating to others.

Affirmations for Dating and Intimacy

We recommend you say these affirmations out loud throughout the day to connect with your intention of a mindful recovery. We also recommend you type one affirmation into your smartphone each morning as a reminder to use it three to five times daily. You can download a printable copy of these affirmations at the website for this book: http://www .newharbinger.com/40705.

Monday: *I reconnect with my breath so that I can be present for myself and others.*

Tuesday: *Each day, I move toward self-forgiveness.*

Wednesday: *I use past experiences as valuable lessons in understanding intimacy.*

Thursday: *Today I trust in my vision for close relationships.*

Friday: *I am mindful of my mental, physical, and spiritual connections with another person.*

Saturday: *I heal myself by taking on new relationships slowly and thoughtfully.*

Sunday: *I honor myself and move away from relationships that do not serve my recovery.*

35

Telling Others About Your Recovery

*It is not necessary to be strong in every place if in the
place you are vulnerable, you are loved.*

—Robert Brault

Pamela liked Colin as soon as she met him. There was an instant
attraction. They were both artists and had a similar way of seeing
things. They both grew up in the Midwest and came from big families.
Once they started dating, Pamela began to feel uneasy about if and
when she should tell Colin about her recovery. Although Pamela had
been clean from prescription painkillers for over a year, she still never
knew the right time to tell other people about her past. It took her six
months to let her brothers and sisters know that she had been abusing
pills. One of her sisters stopped talking to her after that. She tried not
to take the rejection personally, but it left her confused and hurt.
Pamela really cared about Colin. She wanted their relationship to
keep going smoothly.

Have you, like Pamela, also found it hard to tell others about your
recovery? Do you wonder how to do it? By using the mindfulness skills
throughout this book, you already have a great start. Talking about
your recovery will require you to find your center, the place where you
feel resilient and calm. This means that no matter whom you tell or
how others may respond, you can return to your center.

When it's time to tell others about your past, use CENTER as a
reminder that you have an inner space that is 100 percent supportive
of who you are now. CENTER spells out the steps to take.

C: Choose whom you will tell. There is a good chance you will not tell everyone about your addiction and recovery. This is an opportunity to decide whom to tell: your spouse or partner, close friends, casual acquaintances, family members, your boss, your teacher, your coworkers, or that new relationship prospect. Try not to go into too much detail at the beginning. Ask for the person to listen without responding.

E: Expect questions and concerns. Some possible questions to think about before you talk about your recovery are "How long did you use?" "What did you use?" "How long have you been in recovery?" "Did you go into treatment?" "How do I know you won't use again?" If there is a question you are not able to answer right now, you may say, "Let me think about that question and get back to you."

N: Not everyone will understand. If you feel rejected or misunderstood when you tell others about your recovery, remember your feelings are temporary. Acknowledge that they are having feelings of their own, and bring compassion to this space.

T: Timing is everything. With busy schedules, obligations, commitments, and interruptions, it can feel like an impossible task to find the right time to talk. However, you owe it to yourself and your relationship to carve out thirty minutes to focus on this. It may come down to making an appointment for a face-to-face meeting. Please do not tell someone about your recovery in a text or in an e-mail, because this can cause miscommunication. Remember, personal connection is powerful.

E: Empathize with the other person. When someone is addicted, people around that person struggle too. If you are telling someone who is in a relationship with you, your recovery will have an impact on that person too. Be patient with the response you receive, and take a moment to see things from the other person's perspective.

R: Return to your support group. Once you have told someone about your recovery, it's a good idea to reach out to your support network. Doing this allows you to reconnect and refocus on your recovery and reminds you of what you need to be well.

Exercise: Centering Yourself

Before telling another person about your recovery, use this exercise to settle your mind and release any attachment to the outcome. Find a quiet place and allow yourself ten minutes of uninterrupted time. Sit in your favorite chair or on a meditation cushion. If possible, open the window to let fresh air move through the room. If you are outside, notice the air around you. Begin with your breath. Take a few nice deep breaths. Close your eyes. Now, let your recovering mind speak to you. Here is what it is saying to you: *You are good. You are loved. You are whole.* Breathe in and out. Be aware of your breathing. Don't worry about the outcome, or if this feels strange. Return to your center point: the present moment is your center point. Repeat three times *You are good. You are loved. You are whole.* Then change the saying to: *I am good. I am loved. I am whole.* Repeat these three times. Wonderful. You can practice this centering meditation any time. It is especially helpful before and after you plan on telling someone about your recovery. We have faith that you will return to the centered place within yourself on your amazing recovery journey.

Affirmations for Telling Others About Your Recovery

We recommend you say these affirmations out loud throughout the day to connect with your intention of a mindful recovery. We also recommend you type one affirmation into your smartphone each morning as a reminder to use it three to five times daily. You can download a printable copy of these affirmations at the website for this book: http://www .newharbinger.com/40705.

Monday: *I make good decisions about whom I tell about my recovery.*

Tuesday: *Setting the time and place to talk about my recovery increases my well-being.*

Wednesday: *Today I empathize with the person I tell about my recovery.*

Thursday: *I am mindful in returning to my center when I talk about my recovery.*

Friday: *Not everyone will understand. I am okay with that.*

Saturday: *How I think about my recovery helps me communicate with others.*

Sunday: *My wellness depends on being honest with others. I choose the appropriate time.*

SECTION 8

Improving Relationships

36

Communicating Well

Life becomes easier when you learn to accept an apology you never got.

—**Robert Brault**

"When are they going to trust me again? My parents continue to boss me around and think I'm really screwing up. I wish they would stop trying to run my life." Zach knew his parents had a list of things a mile long they wanted to change about him. He wanted to talk to them about how good things were going in his recovery, but he didn't know where to start. The more he tried to tell them about his recovery, the worse the conversation went, until they all would just give up in frustration. Zach wondered how he could get his point across.

You, like Zach, may need a few skills for how to communicate better with others in your life. We have some good news for you: you already have the wisdom to communicate well. This is true, even if you sometimes feel that no one understands you or you are not connecting with others. You have the wisdom you will need to be a great communicator. You have an innate sense of how to communicate, because you know what it feels like to be listened to. It feels good, right? We want you to tap into your wisdom here. We offer five simple tools to practice on a regular basis to boost the wisdom that you have within. Our communication tools spell the word LIGHT, because communicating well requires a light touch.

L: Live in the moment. Be present for what is happening in the here and now. When most of us are in conversation with another person, we are focused either on past disappointments or on future worries. Usually, we have a quick response to what other people are saying, whether or not they have finished talking. You can bring yourself back to the moment with your number one go-to: your breath.

I: Increase your empathy. To empathize with someone is to look at the situation from the other person's perspective. Most misunderstandings in the past felt like the end of the world. Now with a little practice, you are better able to see things from the other person's vantage point. Yes, you can have empathy even if you disagree with someone else's behavior or opinion!

G: Give up teaching lessons. When the focus is on teaching someone else a lesson, you lose focus on yourself, and communicating well requires *self-awareness*. Once you get the idea of no lessons, it frees you up to really listen to the other person. You will be offering support and validation to the other person. If you are asked for advice, of course you may give it. Otherwise, please refrain from teaching.

H: Have patience. One of the things that fell by the wayside in your past addiction was patience. Usually, frustration and agitation took center stage. Now, to communicate well in recovery, you can practice being patient and tolerant with others.

T: Two-way street. It's a good idea to briefly repeat what you heard the other person say so both of you know you are on the right track. Once you have repeated the main point or points, you can then bring in your side of the conversation. Remind yourself that you are practicing communicating well and that it may take a few attempts to feel comfortable with this mindful way of connecting.

Although Zach thought he had tried everything when it came to communicating with his parents, he was open to giving the LIGHT skills a go. When he did, he realized that he hadn't been listening to his parents; when talking, all he did was think about past disappointments and try to teach them lessons. Zach began to be more present with his parents and made every effort to stop teaching. His parents told him they felt understood for the first time. Their communication was going in a great direction.

Try these LIGHT communication practices the next time you interact with someone. Tap into your wisdom, and notice the shifts in your connections.

Exercise: Centering with Standing Mindfulness

This is a standing mindfulness exercise that includes a brief visualization. If you have any difficulty standing for five minutes, you can do this exercise while sitting with your feet planted firmly on the ground.

Find a quiet place with no interruptions for five to eight minutes. Plant your feet firmly on the ground hip-width apart. Look down and make sure your feet are pointed directly out in front of you. Take a moment to straighten your spine and neck. Place your arms by your sides with your palms facing out. Close your eyes. Begin to breathe evenly and slowly. Next, imagine there are roots coming out of the bottom of your feet moving into the earth below. The roots represent your stability and security. Imagine the top of your head reaching for the sky, past the ceiling. The sky represents your wisdom. Notice your breathing. After a few minutes, lift your arms over your head. Reach your fingers up to the sky. Then bring your palms together in a prayer position. Bring your hands together at the center of your chest, your heart center. Your touching hands represent your ability to communicate with compassion. Inhale and exhale. Stay in this posture for a few minutes. When you are ready, open your eyes. By practicing this standing mindfulness posture, you have quieted your mind and centered your body. Light heart, open mind. Nicely done!

Affirmations for Communicating Well

We recommend you say these affirmations out loud throughout the day to connect with your intention of a mindful recovery. We also recommend you type one affirmation into your smartphone each morning as a reminder to use it three to five times daily. You can download a printable copy of these affirmations at the website for this book: http://www.newharbinger.com/40705.

Monday: *I tap into my inner wisdom to communicate well.*

Tuesday: *Slowing down and being present are an important part of how I listen.*

Wednesday: *There is no need to teach anyone a lesson.*

Thursday: *Empathy for the other person is one of my communication practices.*

Friday: *My recovery includes valuing how I communicate with others.*

Saturday: *I allow space in my recovery to be honest in my communication.*

Sunday: *Today I take responsibility for my role in improving communication.*

37

Resolving Conflict Mindfully

Respond; don't react.
Listen; don't talk.
Think; don't assume.

—Raji Lukkoor

"I'm done. I don't want to do this anymore." Jada stopped listening even before Brad could get his side of the story out.

Brad, his face getting red and hot, said, "You always cut me off and shut things down. You never let me get my thoughts out."

Jada yelled, "I really don't care. You lied to me."

As you can guess, this conflict—the back-and-forth of accusations, the not listening, and the name-calling—could go on forever. Jada and Brad are stuck in a power struggle. Emotions have a way of taking over, even when you start out with the intention of just talking. In fact, when you are in conflict with another person, it really means you are out of touch with yourself. Conflict equals personal disconnection. If Jada or Brad had the skills to manage their emotions, and could slow down and listen, their argument might take a different path.

How do you resolve conflicts? In the past, you may have reached for a drink, drug, or other addictive behavior to calm down and take your mind off the problem. That may have worked temporarily, but it also cut you off from playing an active role in your interactions. Now why don't you see if using some mindfulness skills will help the next time you get in a bind with another person? Keep in mind: being in recovery does not mean that all conflicts neatly go away. But you do have alternatives when you bump up against disagreements.

We will break these down into two categories. First, here are some mindfulness-based actions you can take when you are in the heat of conflict. These spell out CHAT.

C: Change your posture. If you notice that you are standing up, sit down. If you are sitting down, move around in your chair, notice the back of the chair against your back, be aware of your arms against the armrests, rub your neck, or uncross your legs. A new position will help you be present in your body.

H: H_2O. Drink water. We recommend the easy, tried-and-true habit of drinking a cool glass of water. Drink slowly with breaks between sips. Water cools down your central nervous system. It also improves brain function, including thinking and mental alertness. And hydrating helps eliminate toxins from the body. Even mild dehydration has been linked to anger, tiredness, problems in thinking, and mood swings in both men (Ganio et al. 2011) and women (Armstrong et al. 2011). So reach for some water, and notice how your body cools down and your thinking improves.

A: Air. Breathe. No need to complicate things here. Breathing always works to help you recenter yourself. As you have learned throughout this book, taking three to five deep breaths will give your mind and body time to calm down. Breathing in the present moment tells your brain that what you are experiencing is not an emergency. So do yourself a favor and take some deep breaths.

T: Time away. The best way to manage conflict is to move away from the situation for a short time. We are not suggesting that you bolt out the door never to return. The most respectful way to manage the conflict is to say, "What you are saying is important to me. Can you give me fifteen minutes [or thirty minutes] to think about it and come back to discuss it with you?" Then go into another room and regroup. Or even better, go outside and take a brief walk.

In addition to these actions, here are some mindfulness-based communication skills you can practice in any interpersonal conflict. They spell out VARY.

V: **Validate the other person's point of view.** You can validate the other person even if you do not agree with what the person is saying. Statements like "I see where you are coming from" and "I understand that you are upset right now" will go a long way to calmly reconnect with the other person.

A: **Ask for the person to repeat.** Sometimes things happen so fast, you might have missed the actual problem. Every situation is unique, even if you feel you have been down this path before. It never hurts to ask the other person to repeat what the problem is so you have a clear understanding of the issue at hand.

R: **Respond with kindness.** Well, we know how challenging it is to feel empathy and kindness when you are feeling offended, angry, hurt, or disappointed. Remember, we are asking you to try these skills on for size. Responding with kindness can be as simple as saying "That must be tough."

Y: **Your role.** Take responsibility for your role in the disagreement. As much as any of us would like to teach someone else a lesson, that usually does not work. You only have control of your own self and your own behavior. You cannot control or change another person's responses. If you are curious about your role, you have a better chance to come upon a peaceful outcome.

You are going to feel awkward, strange, and out of sorts when you start resolving conflicts mindfully. It's guaranteed that you will be out of your comfort zone. But give these practices a try: a mindfulness approach might be your best chance to resolve stubborn conflict.

Exercise: Resolving Conflict Mindfully

For this exercise, we would like you to think about a difficult or uncomfortable interaction with someone.

1. First, review the interpersonal conflict and pay attention to your emotional responses during the experience.

2. Next, review the experience from the other person's point of view. See if you can put yourself in the other person's shoes. What feelings come up? Can you understand where the person is coming from?

3. Now look at the conflict as an observer, as if you were not part of it. Think of yourself as a neutral scientist looking in on the experience. As a scientist, you have no emotion about what is happening; you are just *observing*.

We want you to look at the conflict without reacting to it. This meditation will help you improve your ability to understand the feelings about the event without reacting to those feelings. See if you can reflect on your intentions and the intentions of the other person. Instead of avoiding the conflict or chasing the fight, this is an opportunity to slow down and be aware in the moment. Well done!

Affirmations for Resolving Conflict Mindfully

We recommend you say these affirmations out loud throughout the day to connect with your intention of a mindful recovery. We also recommend you type one affirmation into your smartphone each morning as a reminder to use it three to five times daily. You can download a printable copy of these affirmations at the website for this book: http://www.newharbinger.com/40705.

Monday: *I can slow down and look at this conflict as an observer.*

Tuesday: *Drinking cool water is my go-to when I feel anger rising within me.*

Wednesday: *Today I focus on listening to another, without judgment.*

Thursday: *Reminding myself of my role in conflict allows me to be active in resolving it.*

Friday: *My healthy recovery includes practicing mindful ways to manage conflict.*

Saturday: *I feel better when I respond to conflict with kindness.*

Sunday: *Remaining focused, calm, and present during conflict increases my well-being.*

38

Resentment and Forgiveness

Our failure to know joy is a direct reflection of our inability to forgive.

—**Charlotte Joko Beck**

"That's quite a collection," Jackie said, as she admired the items lined up along Brian's shelves.

"Yeah. Those are all my resentments. I have been collecting them for years," said Brian, who has eight months of sobriety. "This one is from last year. It's my resentment toward my ex-wife for how she treated me. This one here is two years old; it's my resentment from when my boss didn't promote me. That one over there is seven years old," he said pointing to one of his resentments on the top shelf. "That's my resentment from when my brother didn't pay back the money he owed me. And this one is over ten years old. It's my resentment from when my mom didn't come to my wedding."

"Wow." Jackie was impressed. She had her own resentment collection but nothing like this. They both stared at Brian's impressive resentment collection. Then Jackie blurted out, "You'd have a lot more space in here if you got rid of some of these resentments."

"No," Brian said. "I'd rather keep all of them. Besides, I have no idea how to get rid of them."

There is a very good chance that you too have an imposing collection of resentments: feelings of indignant displeasure or persistent ill will at a real or imagined wrong, insult, or injury. These feelings can last for days, years, decades, and even lifetimes. Whether you are harboring a vast collection of resentments or you have just a twinge of anger at being treated unfairly, this is your opportunity to learn about what is fueling your negative feelings.

Resentments are a very real danger to your recovery. Left unattended, these intense feelings of hurt, anger, betrayal, and disappointment can derail you and lead to relapse. The most powerful resentments are usually felt toward someone to whom you were once close, like a spouse, boyfriend, girlfriend, family member, boss, or old friend. You want that person to pay for what he or she did to you. You may have to pretend the feelings are not there when you deal with the person you are angry with. Faking your interactions can lead to feeling out of touch, disconnected, and off-balance. Resentments can get stronger over time.

What impact does resentment have on you? Some people in recovery report feeling on edge, anxious, stressed, and angry. Holding on to resentment can have both short- and long-term effects on you and your physical and emotional well-being. Holding on to resentments also impacts your ability to have healthy relationships. You can see here that resentment has a serious negative effect on you. Surprisingly, your resentment has very little effect on the person you resent.

So the question is, what is the cure? What do you do if, like Brian, you have a lot of resentments? Can you really overcome them? Well, we have a plan. This plan includes the idea of *forgiveness* and letting go of your resentments.

Why should you forgive others who have harmed you? Forgiveness is a gift you will be giving to yourself. It really does not have anything to do with the person you feel resentment toward. We know that sounds strange. We did not say you will be excusing the behavior that may have caused you pain. Rather, we want you to entertain the idea of forgiving both the other person and yourself for the hurt that the behavior may have caused. Let it go.

Forgiveness is a value that is either true for you or not. Once you make the decision to believe in the value of forgiveness, your world will change. Forgiveness is your own personal key to unlock the door to a healthier, happier, calmer, and more joyful you. It is an agreement that you make with yourself that you are worthy of living a life of possibilities. We cannot control what other people do, but we can choose how we react. Now you can choose a response that is in line with your recovery and well-being.

Exercise: Writing Down Resentments and Moving into Forgiveness

This writing exercise is like the fourth step of the 12-step program, which is extremely helpful in recovery. If you are already practicing the 12 steps, this exercise may help you go deeper, learn more about your resentments, and cultivate forgiveness. If you are not working the 12 steps, this exercise may be especially beneficial for you.

Find a quiet space and allow yourself twenty minutes of uninterrupted time. Get out your journal. As you move through answering these questions, take an open and honest look at your experiences. Accept all parts of yourself. All your emotions are deserving of your time and attention.

Write down your answers to these questions:

1. What exactly happened? Write a summary of the event that caused your resentment.

2. What is your role in the resentment? All resentments are interpersonal interactions. Write down any ideas that come to mind about your part in the resentment. This will allow you to make different choices in the future, which can lead to less pain.

3. What emotions do you have about the situation?

4. How was this event like another event where you felt resentment?

5. How has resentment affected you emotionally, physically, and spiritually?

6. What value do forgiving and letting go have for you?

7. How will you feel when you are able to forgive the other person?

You have made a great start at understanding resentment and walking along into forgiveness. If you have many lingering resentments, we recommend you practice this exercise again from the beginning. After all, spending some time with your resentments now may help lessen the collection later. Experiencing the art of forgiveness will move you closer to joy.

Affirmations for Forgiveness

We recommend you say these affirmations out loud throughout the day to connect with your intention of a mindful recovery. We also recommend you type one affirmation into your smartphone each morning as a reminder to use it three to five times daily. You can download a printable copy of these affirmations at the website for this book: http://www.newharbinger.com/40705.

Monday: *Today I will invite moments of forgiveness into my day.*

Tuesday: *I allow resentments to slowly melt away; they are not part of my essential self.*

Wednesday: *Returning to an attitude of forgiveness is healthy for me.*

Thursday: *My heart is big; I can forgive others.*

Friday: *I thank myself for moving toward a spirit of forgiving.*

Saturday: *I know that my recovery journey includes forgiveness.*

Sunday: *Today I am open to learning more about the power of forgiveness.*

The Gift of Recovery

39

Other People's Feelings

The simple act of being completely attentive and present to another person is an act of love, and it fosters unshakable well-being.

—Sharon Salzberg

Recovery comes with its fair share of surprises. One you may have noticed is that your emotions can be on a roller-coaster ride. Sometimes you are on top of the world, and other times you feel like you are in a pit and unable to get out. Or the roller coaster is stalled at the gate: you feel numb to everything and everyone. Most times it's difficult to identify exactly what you are feeling. Over time, with lots of practice—and with help from your sponsor or therapist and from this book—it will get better. But there is still the nagging problem of other people's feelings. Two things can happen when it comes to other people's feelings. Not understanding what other people are feeling is one of them. The other thing that can happen is you feel too much and tend to take on other people's problems as your own.

Missing the Cues

First, if you're not able to read feeling cues, you are not alone. This happens so often in recovery. It sometimes feels like you have *emotional blind spots* when it comes to others; you think you know what they are feeling, but you are off target. You may take a wild guess about what someone is feeling, and, nine times out of ten, you get it wrong. This can get you into trouble with friends, family, and close relationships. This was how Ted, three months clean and sober, interacted with his girlfriend, Abby. He simply could not pick up the cues when Abby was upset, and this made her furious. Other times, he would check out by playing video games for hours, afraid of starting another argument. This avoidance also made things worse. What Ted was experiencing has a name, *alexithymia*, which is when you have no words for emotions, and it is extremely common in recovery from addictions. It's difficult to go through life when you don't have words for emotions. In recovery, you are just getting to know yourself and your own emotions. It's another level of emotional challenge to be aware of other people's feelings.

Without an ability to identify and assess your own emotions, it is exceptionally difficult to decipher the emotions of others. So, here is a two-part practice. The first is to accurately identify your own feelings. Slow down and give your brain time to unpack the problem and the feelings that go along with it. Once you have an accurate reading of your own feelings, you'll be better able to tap into what another person is feeling. You do not need to fix, solve, or make the other person's feelings disappear. We are simply asking you to slow down and notice what is going on without reacting. Check in with the other person. Ask, "What are you feeling right now?" Or, if you are pretty sure you have a good read on the other person's feelings, go ahead and say, "I can see that you are angry, and I can understand that." That last statement has the added component of *empathy*, which is the ability to identify and understand another person's situation. It's the ability to put yourself in another person's shoes. You are developing the ability to understand how your actions impact others. Remember, this will take practice.

Taking on Feelings

The second challenge people in recovery experience is feeling and helping others *too much*. You not only put yourself in other people's shoes but are running the marathon for them. You want to fix all their problems, take the burden off their shoulders, and, in general, meet all their needs. That's a lot to take on.

Taking on other people's feelings was exactly what Carla was trying to change. Carla, five months sober, was known by all her friends as the one to go to with any problem. She would answer her phone at all hours of the night and spend hours every day taking care of other people's feelings. Her friends jokingly called Carla "my favorite shrink."

What effect do you think this approach to other people's feelings has had on your recovery? If you take on other people's feelings, there's a good chance that you will feel resentful or angry, or you may feel drained and depleted. Carla could pick up other people's emotional cues but sorely missed her own. You, too, may have lost track of your own needs. These feelings of exhaustion and disconnection could fuel a lapse into alcohol, drugs, or other risky behaviors.

Checking in with yourself on a regular basis is your best chance to gain back a sense of balance and calm. We're not saying you should completely stop taking care of other people, but it's time to make sure that you take care of yourself too. By establishing personal boundaries, nurturing those relationships that feel healthy, and incorporating some of the mindfulness techniques introduced throughout this book, you are making a commitment to your continued recovery.

Exercise: Writing About Other People's Feelings

Get out your journal and a pen. Find a quiet place to sit, and allow yourself twenty minutes of uninterrupted time. Think about someone who is bothering you or someone you are concerned about. Next, explore your own feelings about this person. Write down this phrase in your journal: *I am aware of myself and my feelings now.* Next, reflect on what feelings the other person may be having. Make a list of some possibilities. Is the other person feeling anger? Frustration? Overwhelmed? Sadness? Joy?

Before you interact with the person in question, reflect on your thoughts and feelings about the situation. Then allow yourself time to interact with the person. Let the person know that you understand what's going on for him or her (remember, you may need to check in to confirm that you have guessed right). Allow yourself time to take care of yourself. Let your friends or family know that you understand what they are feeling (remember, you do not have to fix their feelings). Spend time with your sponsor or others who interact well with others, so you can continue to observe good models.

Affirmations for Other People's Feelings

We recommend you say these affirmations out loud throughout the day to connect with your intention of a mindful recovery. We also recommend you type one affirmation into your smartphone each morning as a reminder to use it three to five times daily. You can download a printable copy of these affirmations at the website for this book: http://www .newharbinger.com/40705.

Monday:	*Today I notice my own feelings. This helps me better understand others.*
Tuesday:	*I look for ways to connect with others in an authentic way.*
Wednesday:	*I check in with someone to make sure I can identify this person's feelings.*
Thursday:	*I set healthy boundaries with others to maintain my own health and recovery.*
Friday:	*Today I pay full attention without reacting to what someone else is saying.*
Saturday:	*I connect with another person and have no expectations.*
Sunday:	*My recovery is stronger when I allow others to have their feelings.*

SECTION 9

Bonding with Your Body

40

Love and Respect for Your Body

The human body is the best work of art.

—Jess C. Scott

"You know how people say, 'My body is a temple?'" Sarah says. "My body was more like a trash can. Junk food, alcohol, sometimes drugs…I tossed it all in without a thought. What did I care? I didn't have much respect for myself when I was using. In recovery, I started to see things differently. I knew I didn't want the health problems my parents had. And I wanted to feel good in my skin. I decided to look at my body like a really nice car. I would take care of a really nice car, right? So I could drive it for a long time. I'd probably polish it, keep it clean. I'd make sure it got regular maintenance—that's like me going to the doctor. This is the one body I've got; there are no trade-ins on this one. I'd like to keep it running smooth. It is worth a little effort. After all I've been through so far, I think I deserve a nice ride!"

If you want to feel well and live well, it is time to treat your body well. Much like Sarah, you may find that during your addiction you developed a bad habit of neglecting or even mistreating your body. You may not have been aware of it. In your addiction, it would have been too horrifying to really let yourself see what you were doing to your body. Your beautiful mind is set up to protect you from that kind of discomfort. It has all kinds of defense mechanisms that keep tough realities at bay, like *denial*, or refusing to see the effects of your lifestyle on your body. You have probably been in denial for a very long time. Now that you are recovering, you will begin to see things clearly. It is time to let go of the illusion that you can disregard your body and still carry on with your life. It is time to make the connection that your body is your life.

Whether you believe in one life, many lives, an afterlife, or no afterlife, the truth is that in this life, in this moment, your body is the only one you have. It is your vehicle, and you cannot get anywhere without it. Imagine for a moment the things you most want to accomplish. What experiences do you most want to have? What brings you the most joy in life? Chances are, everything you just imagined requires your body. Seeing something beautiful, holding someone you love, eating, moving, painting, even daydreaming—remember, your brain is a part of your body, too—all require your healthy body.

Unfortunately, this incredible vehicle of yours is also fragile. It experiences wear and tear under even the best of circumstances. If you want it to carry you far, you must give it the respect it deserves. Most of us don't just want to live long; we want to live well. We would like our minds to stay sharp and our bodies to stay strong. Think about it: the way you treat your body matters.

It is never too late to make a change in how you treat your body. Use the following exercise to get closer to your body and find the inspiration to treat your body well!

Exercise: Practicing Love and Respect for Your Body

This is a writing exercise. Find a comfortable place to sit with your journal and a favorite pen. Begin by closing your eyes and breathing slowly. Let the air flow deep into the belly and release smoothly as you exhale. Offer an intention to be present for this experience.

Now it is time to approach your body with gratitude. Consider all that it does for you. Think of all that it is capable of and all that it provides. For each part of your body, list as many things as you can think of to be grateful for. For example, you may write *Eyes: watching the sunset, seeing my daughter smile, watching a movie. I get to see all these* beautiful colors… or *Hands: thank you for buttoning my shirts. I love holding hands with my nephew. I like driving and holding the steering wheel…*

You may list reasons to be grateful for as many or as few parts of the body as you like. Maybe you will write about your teeth, tongue, ears, heart, lungs, stomach, spine, knees, toes, colon, liver, bones, blood… the list goes on and on. Let yourself be in genuine awe and gratitude for all that your body does for you. You may find a strong desire to treat it well in return!

Affirmations for Love and Respect for your Body

We recommend you say these affirmations out loud throughout the day to connect with your intention of a mindful recovery. We also recommend you type one affirmation into your smartphone each morning as a reminder to use it three to five times daily. You can download a printable copy of these affirmations at the website for this book: http://www .newharbinger.com/40705.

Monday: *I am my body; my body is me.*

Tuesday: *I treat my body with the love and respect it deserves.*

Wednesday: *I am grateful for my body in recovery.*

Thursday: *Today I offer love and kindness to my body.*

Friday: *Thank you, body, for all that you offer me.*

Saturday: *I treat my body as I would treat my best friend.*

Sunday   *In this life, this is the only body I have. I treat my body well and I deserve to live well.*

41

Prioritizing Sleep

Without enough sleep, we all become tall two-year-olds.

—JoJo Jensen

People in recovery from addiction will be the first to tell you that their sleep is a mess. Whether it's not being able to fall asleep, waking up at all hours of the night, or bolting awake in the wee hours of the morning— getting a good night's sleep feels just about impossible. Sometimes an avalanche of thoughts comes tumbling into your mind right as you turn off the light. Or maybe you are someone who has recurring bad dreams that rob you of precious rest. Many people in recovery have dreams where they are using drugs, drinking, or engaging in other destructive behaviors, which can be extremely unsettling.

If you are experiencing any of these sleep problems, most likely you will be exhausted, both physically and emotionally. And feeling exhausted will only intensify any mood problems, like anxiety or depression, you may be having. Allowing the mind and body to rest and enjoy a good night's sleep is the final frontier in the recovery journey.

How Addiction Affects Sleep

Even if you have been sober for months or years, quality sleep can still be difficult to achieve because addiction robs your brain of the mechanism it needs to rest and fall asleep. In the past, you may have used alcohol or drugs to try to get some sleep on restless nights, but the opposite effect most likely happened. For instance, alcohol may have a temporary sedative effect, but that effect wears off as soon as the alcohol leaves the body, usually around two o'clock in the morning. Smoking cigarettes also has a bad effect on your sleep (Zhang et al. 2006). Did you know that people who smoke a pack of cigarettes a day can lose up to twenty minutes of sleep at night?

Chronic insomnia, or not getting sleep over a period, has been shown to be one of the most common side effects in people with drug and alcohol problems. Insomnia is such an unpleasant experience, it can be a trigger for relapsing to drugs or alcohol. A study in the *Journal of Addiction Medicine* (Kaplan et al. 2014) found that insomnia is five times higher in people in recovery than in the general population. This study also uncovered evidence that insomnia can predict relapse in people in recovery. Well, now that we have this information, it's clear that prioritizing sleep will help with sustaining your recovery and may help prevent relapse. You will need to make some changes here, but making your sleep a priority can have lasting positive consequences.

We recommend that you talk to your health care provider about your sleep problems or any changes in sleep that you are experiencing, and let your health care provider know that you are in recovery! Next, we have some tips for how to prioritize sleep. As you read through these tips, notice your reactions to them. If you have negative thoughts like *I'm never going to get decent sleep, I ruined my brain by drinking and using all those years, My busy life does not allow for these changes,* or *Having a regular sleep schedule is boring, no thanks,* allow your thoughts in and allow them to move on. Your mind is working overtime to keep things the same as they have always been.

Exercise: Relearning Sleep

Entertain the idea of trying new behaviors on the road to healthy sleep. Now is the time to make room for sleep. Use this phrase to calm down: *I choose healthy ways to improve my sleep.* Here is an easy way to remember these tips: SLEEP.

S: Schedule sleep. A regular sleep schedule is your friend when your goal is better sleep. Going to bed and waking up at the same time on weekdays and weekends will help regulate your body's clock. This is the tip people fight with the most, especially the weekend schedule. Give it a try and notice how you feel.

L: Lower the lights. Thirty to sixty minutes before your bedtime, go around your home and lower the lights. This means turning off all electronic equipment, computers, tablets, cellphones, and televisions. The purpose is to decrease the activities that excite the brain. In addition, lower the lights in your bedroom. This will give your mind and body permission to unplug and slow down: a welcome reprieve from your busy, plugged-in day.

E: Exercise. Yes, that means you. Doing light to moderate exercise daily can have a significant impact on your body's ability to rest at the end of the day. Walking after work for twenty minutes is a nice way to start. Yoga and light stretching have been shown to have positive restful effects on both the body and the mind (Wei and Groves 2017). Find an activity that you enjoy, or branch out and try a new exercise in your effort to prioritize sleep. Avoid doing strenuous exercise close to bedtime.

E: Evaluate your room. Is there is a loud ticking clock near your bed? Is your cellphone constantly pinging? Is your bedroom too bright even with the shades drawn? Evaluate if your bedroom is the comfortable, dark, quiet place you need to rest and improve your sleep. Move your cellphone out of the bedroom or turn it off (trust us with this one), get blackout shades, and move any ticking clock out of your bedroom. Use a quiet digital clock to set your alarm to wake up. Small changes will make a big difference.

P: Pillows and mattresses. If you're like most of us, you may have a mattress or pillows that are over a decade old. To prioritize your sleep, it may be time to invest in a new supportive mattress and a high-quality pillow. Think of this financial investment as an investment in your overall recovery.

Remember, in recovery you will need to take extra care of your sleep life. You won't be able to catch up on all the missed or disrupted sleep in your past, but with a few changes you can make SLEEP a priority for long-term health and well-being.

Affirmations for Prioritizing Sleep

We recommend you say these affirmations out loud throughout the day to connect with your intention of a mindful recovery. We also recommend you type one affirmation into your smartphone each morning as a reminder to use it three to five times daily. You can download a printable copy of these affirmations at the website for this book: http://www.newharbinger.com/40705.

Monday: *Throughout the day, I allow myself moments of rest.*

Tuesday: *Sleep comes naturally to me this evening.*

Wednesday: *Relaxation before sleep enhances my ability to move into sleep.*

Thursday: *I feel safe and I can let myself relax at night.*

Friday: *I notice my thoughts about sleep and let them go, without judgment.*

Saturday: *My environment is a wonderful setting to fall into a restful sleep.*

Sunday: *I release any worries about tomorrow and focus on enjoying this moment of rest.*

42

Mindful Eating

The more you eat, the less flavor; the less you eat, the more flavor.

—Chinese proverb

Connie has been sober for almost eight months. She feels a lot better than when she was drinking, but she still finds herself feeling sluggish and unmotivated a lot of the time. Maybe it has something to do with her eating, she wonders. At lunch, she eats at her desk, hardly taking her eyes off her work. When she gets home at night, stressed, she goes right to the fridge. She gets the feeling that eating a bag of cookies every night isn't helping with her energy.

For most people, when it comes to our eating, the word mindful does not apply. Mindless is usually a better fit. Eating can become another way of avoiding, suppressing, or attempting to soothe your uncomfortable feelings. But when you try to use food to address problems other than hunger, the problems go unsolved. For many, food itself becomes addictive. Much like your other addictive behaviors, food plays the tricky game of actually working for a while. It does serve a soothing function. It can be a nice distraction or a way of relieving stress. But like all addictive behaviors, its dark side is lurking.

When food becomes a substance you use to cope, instead of the fuel your body uses to thrive, you are likely to feel sluggish. You are also likely to gain weight. Eating based on how you feel emotionally, instead of what you need physically, usually leads to poor food choices. (Let's face it: you don't reach for the broccoli to unwind.) When you aren't mindful of your body's cues, you lose track of when you are full, and you overeat. Feeling sluggish, tired, and heavy is not a recipe for the thriving recovery you seek.

Give yourself the chance to eat mindfully. Choose to be present for the experience of eating. You can learn to notice and attend to your hunger and fullness cues and to choose foods that really nourish you. You can learn to eat without distractions (no TV, no cell phone, and no loud anxious thoughts). This may be a strange, new concept in the world of fast, mindless, emotional eating. But as with all your new skills, it is worth a try!

Eating mindfully is also a gateway to greater mindfulness overall. Most of us eat three meals a day. That gives you three reminders to pause and bring your attention to exactly where you are and what you are doing. Acknowledge that you are here to nourish your body. This is truly an act of self-care. Breathe deeply and be here now, in this moment, while you eat.

Exercise: Practicing Mindful Eating

This exercise is a classic introduction to mindful eating called "Eating on Another Planet" (Bays 2009). You will need a small piece of food, such as a raisin, a cracker, or a grape.

Place the food in front of you and close your eyes. While breathing slowly, bring your awareness to your imagination. Imagine that you have just landed on a strange new planet. The air is fresh and clear, and breathing is easy here. You are hungry, though, and need to find something to eat. It is time to go exploring. Open your eyes. Notice the item in front of you. You have never seen this item before, and you don't know if it is safe. You approach the item with caution and curiosity, using your five senses as a guide.

Begin by exploring the object with your eyes. Notice its color, its shape, and its size. Use your eyes to explore its texture. Does it have any unique markings?

Now you decide to pick the object up. Place the object in the palm of your hand. Poke it with your finger. Roll it over. Experience the weight of it and notice its surface. Does it feel the way you imagined it would when you first looked at it?

Now smell the object. Place it near your nose and deeply inhale. Then move it away and take another breath before smelling the object again. What do you notice about the smell? Is it strong or light? Does the smell make you want to taste this item?

Next, place the object in your mouth without biting it. Explore the object with your tongue. Move it around in your mouth. Notice its textures and any tastes you experience. How does your mouth respond to this new object?

Now take a bite. Just one. Notice the sensations that arise in your mouth when you take this one bite. Notice what happens to the object when you bite into it. Roll it around in your mouth again.

Finally, begin to chew slowly. Notice the sensations that arise as you chew. Bring your attention to how the object changes as you chew. Swallow the object and then explore your mouth with your tongue. What has the object left behind? How long can you taste the flavor of this object after you have swallowed it?

You have just had a truly mindful eating experience! While it may be hard to do this with every bite of food, you can make a lot of progress in mindful eating by noticing the shapes and colors on your plate before you start eating, pausing to smell a bite of food before you eat it, and putting your fork down between bites to give yourself the chance to chew and taste each bite before you move on to the next one. Be present as you nourish and fuel your body. Bon appétit!

Affirmations for Mindful Eating

We recommend you say these affirmations out loud throughout the day to connect with your intention of a mindful recovery. We also recommend you type one affirmation into your smartphone each morning as a reminder to use it three to five times daily. You can download a printable copy of these affirmations at the website for this book: http://www.newharbinger.com/40705.

Monday: *Today I am present for the experience of eating.*

Tuesday: *I choose to nourish my body by bringing my attention to my food.*

Wednesday: *Mindful eating is an important part of my experience of wellness.*

Thursday: *I enjoy the pleasures of eating mindfully in my recovery.*

Friday: *I engage with the sights, smells, and flavors of each bite of my food.*

Saturday: *I bring my love and attention to the act of eating.*

Sunday: *Today I will be mindful of my hunger and my fullness. Food is my fuel.*

43

Mindful Movement

Walk as if you are kissing the Earth with your feet.

—**Thich Nhat Hanh**

Evan's routine was just not working. He always seemed to get up late, rush through his shower, and quickly leave the house for the local coffee shop. Standing in line for coffee with a bunch of other stressed-out people, Evan felt himself getting more and more agitated. He got to work fifteen minutes late and started most days tense and frustrated. Evan used to smoke pot to take the edge off, and even after six months without it, he felt physically and mentally tight. His body and mind felt disconnected, and he wanted to figure out how not to rush through his day.

If you are someone who runs around all day like Evan does, unaware of your body or your surroundings and stressed out, mindful movement may be just the thing for you. Mindful movement is the experience of bringing your mindfulness practice into the movement of your body. The purpose is to bring awareness to your body and your simple everyday movements, which can help steady your mood and give you a little more peace.

When you were addicted, you may have just wanted to feel better or to numb the way you were feeling. You may have paid little (or no) attention to your body or to what your physical body needed to be well. Now, in recovery, you have a wonderful opportunity to really listen to your body. This may be the first time you have ever focused attention on your physical movements. Slowing down in this way and paying attention to your body are incredibly powerful. Being aware of your body allows you to experience the vital connection between your mind and your body. See how you feel after practicing mindful movement. Here is an easy step-by-step approach to follow.

Exercise: Moving Mindfully

The first step is to *release any judgment of your body* and what it can and cannot do. (And please release any judgment of mindful movement, too!) You may feel a bit awkward at first. That is normal. We are asking you to shift down from the busy, nonstop, day-to-day rushing around that you're used to doing and to become aware of your movements.

The second step is to *choose an activity* to bring mindful movement to. Start with something simple, for example, taking a walk in your yard, your neighborhood, or a local park and noticing your body. Bring awareness of your feet against the ground. Notice your legs moving you forward. Notice your arms swaying back and forth. Notice your head and neck. Blink. Notice your environment, pay attention to what you see, and become aware of what you smell along the way. You might even notice a sense of peace come over your body.

Evan decided to wake up thirty minutes earlier and try this mindful walking activity. He was surprised at how good he felt during his walks and throughout the day. Another simple activity is to bring mindfulness to the act of doing the dishes. Notice the water on your hands, and feel the temperature of the water. Pay attention to how you are standing and to your legs and feet. Notice how you are breathing as you take care of this ordinary task. Rather than trying to get through this chore as quickly as possible, slow down and breathe. You may notice your mind calming down as you do the dishes. You might even notice yourself smile.

The third step is to decide if you will *expand your mindful movement* to a local class. If you have noticed yoga, Pilates, or tai chi classes in your neighborhood, it may be a good time to take your mindful movement to the next level. Let an instructor be your guide. But remember, the purpose of mindful movement is simply to become more aware of your body, so if you are unable to get to a class, you can continue to regularly practice simple mindful movements on your own to reduce stress and slow down. The intention here is to bring mindful movement into each day and to center yourself in the present moment. Give your body a chance to enjoy your recovering life too.

Affirmations for Mindful Movement

We recommend you say these affirmations out loud throughout the day to connect with your intention of a mindful recovery. We also recommend you type one affirmation into your smartphone each morning as a reminder to use it three to five times daily. You can download a printable copy of these affirmations at the website for this book: http://www.newharbinger.com/40705.

Monday: *I move mindfully throughout my day.*

Tuesday: *Taking a class in mindful movement enhances my recovery.*

Wednesday: *I experience peace and tranquility when I am aware of my body movements.*

Thursday: *Paying attention to simple everyday tasks allows me to relax.*

Friday: *Slowing down and noticing my body helps me stay in the moment.*

Saturday: *Today I have decided not to rush. I am aware of my activities.*

Sunday: *My intention is to reconnect with my body, without judgment.*

44

Yoga and Recovery

It is the greatest manifestation of power to be calm.

—Swami Vivekananda

Vivian was in her first year of recovery when a friend's mother invited her to a yoga class. She thought yoga was just easy, boring stretching. What was the big deal? Nothing like the fast-paced, nonstop life she was living. She decided to go to a class to say that she'd tried yoga and it didn't do anything for her. The class was harder than she thought it would be, her mind raced, and her body did not want to cooperate. But after the class, a wonderful feeling came over Vivian. She felt calm and stress-free for the first time in a long time. The mental chatter had slowed down, and the drama of her day didn't seem important. Vivian couldn't wait to take another class.

Like Vivian, you may enjoy the benefits of yoga too. *Yoga* means "to join." Here we're talking about joining mind, body, and spirit with the goal of calming the rush of negative thoughts, difficult feelings, and physical discomfort. Although you may have noticed yoga studios popping up in your neighborhood, yoga has been around for thousands of years. Originally from India, yoga has gained popularity because people experience benefits from practicing it.

Most addiction recovery programs offer some type of yoga or body awareness program, because people in recovery often have many unaddressed emotional, physical, and spiritual challenges. Many people in recovery are struggling with mental health concerns or past abuse. Others are overcome by back pain, headaches, joint pain, or other physical difficulties. Some people in recovery report losing their spiritual connection.

Now that the sedatives, painkillers, amphetamines, alcohol, other chemicals, and destructive behaviors are no longer being used to combat your mental, physical, or spiritual pain, you will need something else to manage the discomfort. For many, turning to yoga offers some relief. Science has shown that yoga is especially helpful in the regulation of the stress hormones cortisol and adrenaline. If you have high levels of these stress hormones coursing throughout your body, you will not feel good at all. You may even experience high levels of anxiety and worry, and you will want to use substances or engage in an addictive behavior to attempt to decrease these intensely unpleasant feelings. Yoga, a practice of mind-and-body awareness, can be your new go-to as you begin to heal or as you continue on your healing journey.

In recovery, yoga is about reconnecting with yourself, recommitting to your health, and realigning with what matters most to you. Yoga is about building resiliency, releasing blocks, and connecting with your strength. There are only two ways this is accomplished. The first is *to show up*. Give yourself a chance to see how yoga works for your recovery; taking classes on a regular basis will help you figure out where yoga fits in (please check in with your doctor prior to starting any exercise program). The second way this is accomplished is *to breathe*. Yes, it's really that simple. In yoga, it's all about stepping onto your mat and focusing on the breath. If things get tough or if you have cravings that appear out of nowhere, you can always return to yoga postures, and you always have your breath to come back to. Breath is your self-care package. It's 100 percent yours and 100 percent wonderful.

Start with this next counting-your-breath exercise today and throughout the week. You can do it at work, in the car, during a busy commute, or at home. No one needs to know but you. This exercise will be in your recovery toolbox to recalibrate your mood, to heal your body, and to activate your peace of mind in recovery.

Exercise 1: Counting Your Breath

This breathing exercise is best practiced in a quiet space at first. Once you have practiced it a few times, you can use it during stressful times wherever you are. Here we go. Breathe in through your nose for a count of four. Hold the breath for a count of two. Breathe out through your nose for a count of six. Try this breathing exercise three times in a row. When you feel good at it, try it six times in a row.

Take this counting-breath exercise with you, and use it when strong emotions arise. For example, if you feel frustrated at work or in a group setting, take a moment to reconnect with your breath by practicing this exercise. Notice what happens. Do things slow down a bit? Can you calm your mind, even if it's just for a few moments? Are you able to quiet the craving or the negative thought?

Exercise 2: Taking a Yoga Class

Once you have practiced the counting-breath exercise for a while, the next step is to decide if you want to join a yoga class. Remember, in yoga you will be able to join breath with mindful movement. (Getting your doctor's okay is the first step.) If you are new to yoga or if you are returning after a long break, it's wise to take a beginning class. Find a yoga center close to your home or your workplace. Some centers have a week of free classes you can take advantage of. Look online or ask at the front desk about it. Some yoga centers even have child care available. Let the instructor know that you are just starting out.

If you have been a yoga practitioner in the past, now is a good time to reengage with your health and venture to another class. If you have been practicing yoga for a while, it may be time to bring a new sense of enjoyment to your practice or to add another class to your week. Remember, this is about bonding with your body to tap into all-embracing recovery through body, mind, and spirit.

Affirmations for Understanding Yoga and Recovery

We recommend you say these affirmations out loud throughout the day to connect with your intention of a mindful recovery. We also recommend you type one affirmation into your smartphone each morning as a reminder to use it three to five times daily. You can download a printable copy of these affirmations at the website for this book: http://www.newharbinger.com/40705.

Monday: *Today I spend time practicing yoga postures.*

Tuesday: *My body, mind, and spirit are connected.*

Wednesday: *Breathing and releasing stress is my way to take care of myself.*

Thursday: *I allow myself the time to take a yoga class.*

Friday: *My recovery includes breath-and-movement practice.*

Saturday: *It's okay to take a beginning yoga class to calm my mind.*

Sunday: *I invite the power of yoga into my recovery.*

SECTION 10

Values and Self-Worth

45

Knowing Your Worth

I'm awake; I am in the world—I expect no further assurance.

—Louise Glück

"I had no idea what my drinking was doing to my self-esteem," Cara says. "I saw myself as the family failure. The mess. For years, I thought my brother was so successful and my sister was so happy because they were simply better people than I was. I thought I was too stupid or too lazy or too broken to have good things in my life. When I stepped out of my addiction, it was like a fog began to lift. Little by little, I'm feeling better about myself. I'm amazed at what I can do when I'm not hung over all the time! This is the kind of confidence I never found at the bottom of a bottle. I want to have a wonderful life, I'm capable of creating it, and I know now that I deserve it as much as anybody else."

Addiction wreaks havoc on your self-esteem. Your sense of self-worth may be crippled by shame and regret. Like Cara, you may suffer from the illusion that other people are more capable or more deserving than you are. Or maybe you have developed a big ego instead; that's one way people cover up their insecurities. Healthy, happy recovery includes casting off your old misleading beliefs. It is time to develop a true, balanced sense of your own value.

The term *right-sized* is commonly used in recovery, and it means understanding that you are no better and no worse than anyone else. Most of us walk around feeling either better than or less than other people. You may swing from one extreme to the other, with beliefs like *If I'm not first, I'm last* or *If I'm not the best, I'm the worst*. Sometimes you may even compare yourself with yourself, with thoughts like *I'm so much heavier than I used to be* or *Remember that nice car I used to drive?*

Thoughts like these are judgments, and they are not helpful to your recovery or well-being. Healthy self-esteem does not need to compare itself with others. It does not judge others and find itself superior or judge itself and find itself lacking. Knowing your worth and being right-sized means understanding that you have the same right to peace, happiness, kindness, and respect as everyone else in the world.

Buddha has been quoted as saying "You yourself, as much as anybody in the entire universe, deserve your love and affection." You do not need to earn your place in the world. You do not need to create your value. You are entitled to your share of all that is good in this world. No more, no less. You are a person of worth and value, simply because you exist.

It may be hard to become right-sized, to truly know that you have worth, no matter what. As with all your new skills, go ahead and gift yourself with practice! Repeat your affirmations until they begin to edge out those negative, unhelpful thoughts. Notice when your mind gets muddied by better-than or less-than thinking, and see how this affects your self-esteem. Take hold of the fundamental truth that you are a person of value.

Exercise 1: Catching Better-Than and Less-Than Thinking

Give yourself about thirty minutes of uninterrupted time. Sit quietly with your journal and begin with several slow, deep breaths.

In your journal, make a list of ten to fifteen people. These can be people you are close to, people you barely know, or even celebrities you have never met.

Next, ask yourself how you compare yourself with these people. Write the words "better than" or "less than" next to each person, and explain how you have established these judgments. For example, you might say, *My sister: better than, because I'm a better cook and a better dresser than she is.* You might add *less than, because she is in better shape than I am, and she makes more money.*

Continue this process with each person on your list. Once you have become clear about your judgments and have put them on paper, it is time to release them. For each person on your list, repeat aloud: *I am no better than* _____ . *I am no less than* _____ . *I create my value from within. I am at peace with myself as I am today.* Repeat these phrases three times for each person on your list. Repeat this process at least once a day for the next week.

Exercise 2: Treating a Plant with Kindness and Care

For this exercise, you will buy yourself a living plant. Choose a plant that is appropriate to your climate or one that can live inside. Read about this plant; learn about it. Find out what it will need to grow. You will need to pay attention to your plant, giving it some attention each day. Tend to your plant and honor it as a living creature, no better and no worse than any other. Treat it with kindness, respect, and care, as you would like to be treated yourself. Notice how this feels.

Affirmations for Knowing Your Worth

We recommend you say these affirmations out loud throughout the day to connect with your intention of a mindful recovery. We also recommend you type one affirmation into your smartphone each morning as a reminder to use it three to five times daily. You can download a printable copy of these affirmations at the website for this book: http://www .newharbinger.com/40705.

Monday: *Today I release all judgments about myself.*

Tuesday: *External factors do not determine my value; I am valuable because I exist.*

Wednesday: *Through my meditative practice, I come to know my worth.*

Thursday: *Today I notice my judgments of others. I let my judgments float away on my breath.*

Friday: *I am a person of worth and value; I know this to be true.*

Saturday: *I am no better than and no less than anyone else in the world.*

Sunday: *In my mindful recovery, I become right-sized.*

46

Discovering What You Value

Open your arms to change, but don't let go of your values.

—Dalai Lama

"Live Your Values!" Kevin passed this poster on the way to his office every morning. He had no idea what the heck it meant. The phrase just made him angry and anxious. Kevin had no clue what his values were, and he certainly didn't know how to "live" them. But rather than be agitated each morning before work, Kevin decided to take some time to figure out what his values were, now that he was in recovery. But where to start? It's tough to figure out what you value, especially when life has been chaotic for so long.

Values provide you with a sense of direction, a way to make healthy decisions, and a place to come back to when you feel confused and discouraged. When things get tough or you have a difficult decision to make, returning to your values will set you on the right path. Values also help with figuring out what is most important to you, especially when you have so many choices in front of you. When your thoughts and actions are not in sync with your values, things start to feel uncomfortable and unstable. It's a red flag. You may be at risk for taking a path that is not in your best interest.

Your values, whether you know exactly what they are right now or not, are a natural part of you. These are rules of living that were important to you in the past but may have gotten lost when you were active in your addiction. Values are how you treat yourself and others and how you expect others to treat you. Now that you have mental clarity, you can reclaim lost values, and even add some new ones that fit with the person you are now. Your values will be the foundation you can build your life on now. They will help guide you in challenging times and in good times.

Your values are like your fingerprints in that they are unique to you. Take some time with the exercise below to discover or rediscover what you value. This is not a time for judgment or criticism; it's a time to reconnect with the part of you that is looking out for what is best for you now.

Exercise: Discovering What You Value

This is a writing exercise. Find a quiet place with few interruptions, and give yourself fifteen good minutes to commit to this exercise. Take out your journal or notebook and your favorite pen. At the top of the page write: *These are my values.* Then list your values below. Some of these values may have come to mind as you read this book. Others may have come to mind as you listened to your peers in Anonymous meetings. Some you may have already discussed with a counselor, a partner, a sponsor, or a friend. Some you may have heard in your place of worship. What you write down does not need to be a complete list. You can add to it over time.

We have provided a list of eighty values to reflect on as you work on your list. See if any of these values resonate with you. Jot down the ones you like, and pass by the ones you don't like. Ready?

acceptance, appreciation, awareness, balance, belief, calmness, clarity, communication, community, compassion, confidence, connection, courage, creativity, curiosity, dependability, determination, devotion, discipline, empathy, excellence, fairness, family, forgiveness, friendship, fun, generosity, grace, gratitude, growth, happiness, harmony, health, honesty, hope, improvement, insightfulness, integrity, intuition, joy, kindness, knowledge, leadership, love, loyalty, mercy, nature, nonjudgment, nourishment, openness, optimism, passion, peace, persistence, playfulness, positivity, prayer, prosperity, quality, relationships, respect, self-awareness, self-compassion, self-reliance, serenity, service, simplicity, stability, support, teamwork, togetherness, tolerance, trust, truth, understanding, unity, vision, well-being, wisdom, work

Now, take a breath here. Slow down. Inhale and exhale. Next, we would like you to circle the top five values on your list. For example, Kevin's top five values were honesty, optimism, forgiveness, service, and family. He sat with these five values for a few minutes and felt a sense of peace. He felt like he had a foundation. His five values set the groundwork for helping him reconnect with himself and his family.

Look at your top five values and reflect on how you will live with your values in mind. Carry your values with you each day. Have the intention to connect with yourself with your values in mind, to make decisions with your values in mind, and to interact with others with your values in mind. You have now discovered or reclaimed your values! What a wonderful way to be in the world.

Affirmations for Discovering What You Value

We recommend you say these affirmations out loud throughout the day to connect with your intention of a mindful recovery. We also recommend you type one affirmation into your smartphone each morning as a reminder to use it three to five times daily. You can download a printable copy of these affirmations at the website for this book: http://www.newharbinger.com/40705.

Monday: *Today I identify and explore what I value.*

Tuesday: *Focusing on what I value helps me in recovery.*

Wednesday: *My top values guide my interactions today.*

Thursday: *Reminding myself of what I value guides my decisions.*

Friday: *I feel calm and centered when I align with my values.*

Saturday: *My relationships are strong when I am true to my values.*

Sunday: *Being in touch with what I value is how I choose to live my life.*

47

Being Money Mindful

Nothing is left to you at this moment but to have a good laugh!

—**Zen saying**

Money. Not too many things produce as much stress in recovery as this. Not having enough, spending too much, borrowing too often, losing it, earning it, needing it, obsessing over it, or arguing about it. Money always seems to sneak back into your mind. And when you were in your addiction, chances are you burned through money without even thinking about it. Hey, it costs a lot of money to be addicted to something.

You probably have an idea of the cost addiction had on your relationships, health, and spirit. But you may not have thought about addiction's financial cost. The price of using alcohol or drugs, in addition to lost wages, lost jobs, cost of treatment, and even legal costs, can be staggering. We don't want you to beat yourself up about money. But it won't help you to shy away from thinking about the numbers either. Information is power.

Someone who drank daily may have spent from $3,650 to $7,300 a year for many years. A pack-a-day cigarette smoker can spend from $1,900 to $4,000 a year—if you smoked cigarettes for decades, that could reach up to $100,000! It's tougher to estimate the cost of illegal drugs. Conservative estimates say that pot users can spend over $1,000 annually, and methamphetamine users can easily spend $4,000 a year. A person struggling with gambling addiction can be taken down financially by the addictive behavior, losing everything and destroying relationships with family and friends in the process. You get the picture. Now, with mindfulness and self-awareness, you have an opportunity to turn things around. We are with you on the path to developing a new mindful experience with money.

Many of us learned—or didn't learn—about money from our parents. Perhaps your parents were stressed about money, or perhaps no one ever talked about money. It was a big family secret. You might have picked up strange or negative messages about money as a kid, or maybe everything was okay growing up, and you are surprised at how your financial world has collapsed. Whatever you witnessed growing up, you now have a chance to let it go and start a new exciting relationship with your finances. Once negative feelings around money are released, more space will be created to attract that which you desire. This is a more optimistic and compassionate approach to your finances than you may have experienced in the past. You get to look at your choices around money with honesty and awareness. The goal here is to move from surviving to thriving.

Exercise: Experiencing Money Mindfully

Here is a five-step plan to improve how you feel about money. These practices spell out MONEY, which makes them easy to remember.

M: **Mindfully accept where you are now financially.** Whether you are on solid footing or on shaky ground, be kind to yourself. This is not the time to fight with yourself. Breathe. Inhale and exhale. Say to yourself, I value my relationship with money. I am in the present moment with my relationship with money. A few compassionate words to yourself go a long way here. Very nice. Proceed to the next practice.

O: **Open your mind to new opportunities.** As you begin to slow down and become aware of your relationship with money, you might be surprised that opportunities will naturally come your way. Opportunities tend to arrive when you are less stressed and more curious. Give yourself a chance to experience a new opportunity in your life and in your recovery. Wonderful. Move on to the next practice.

N: Notice what you have. Gratitude for what you have in the here and now is so powerful. Take a moment and look around you right now. Reflect on your blessings and your internal strength. Your gratitude could be for small things like *I am grateful for this cup of coffee*. Or your gratitude could be for big things like *I am grateful for paying my rent*. Breathe. You can stay with this practice for as long as you need to. When you are ready, step into the next practice.

E: Educate yourself. Most of us have had no classes on money management. Many of us have gone through life on spending-autopilot. How are we supposed to understand the flow and creation of wealth without some knowledge? Give yourself permission to take a class, read a book, or join a group that focuses energy on learning about finances. Please value yourself and your journey by educating yourself. It's up to you here. Okay. You are prepared for the final practice.

Y: Yes or no. You will be making healthy decisions about money going forward. Sometimes you will be able to say yes to a financial choice, if it is in the best interest of your emotional, spiritual, and recovery health. Other times you will be saying no to a financial choice, if it does not nourish who you are now. If you don't know the answer, slow down and breathe. If someone asks you for financial help, you can say, *I will need to think about that. Let me get back to you.* This allows you to reconnect with yourself and make a decision that matches your values.

Congratulations! You are now firmly on the path to developing a mindful relationship with money. What will you do with your newfound abundance?

Affirmations on Being Money Mindful

We recommend you say these affirmations out loud throughout the day to connect with your intention of a mindful recovery. We also recommend you type one affirmation into your smartphone each morning as a reminder to use it three to five times daily. You can download a printable copy of these affirmations at the website for this book: http://www .newharbinger.com/40705.

Monday:	*I create a life of freedom and opportunities.*
Tuesday:	*Today I respect my relationship with money.*
Wednesday:	*Being aware of money is a way to show kindness to myself.*
Thursday:	*I choose to slow down and breathe when I am nervous about money.*
Friday:	*I have enough money for my needs today.*
Saturday:	*I manifest that which is best for my higher self.*
Sunday:	*Connecting my recovery to my financial goals is powerful.*

48

Reconnecting to Work

Let the beauty of what you love be what you do.

—**Rumi**

Some days Erica has to drag herself out of bed. She angrily slams her alarm clock off at 6:30 a.m. *Ugh. Monday.* She knows she should be grateful for her job, but she just feels dread walking into work. She has lost track of what she likes about her job. She feels like her boss, her coworkers, and her clients constantly need something from her. Erica is burned out and exhausted. When she felt this way in the past, she relapsed.

If you are like Erica and feel dog-tired at work, you may have lost your connection to work or to being a valued worker. If you spend forty or more hours a week at work, it should come as no surprise that finding meaning in work will be a significant part of your successful recovery. We prefer to define *work* as an activity that provides you with a sense of purpose and life direction. Work provides you with lots of benefits in recovery. Of course, it feels good to be financially stable, especially if you have had a period of unemployment. It also feels great to take care of yourself and your family. Focusing on your goals now that you are in recovery and making headway toward accomplishing them is wonderful.

Work has other benefits too. Many people find that working increases their self-confidence and pride; it gives them a sense of a job well done. Others find that they really enjoy the interactions with coworkers, clients, and supervisors that work provides. After talking about her work stress with a counselor, Erica tapped into some of the benefits of work and reconnected with her personal goals. She pressed her work reset button. It felt good for people to count on her. Erica took moments to relax, reconnected with her support system, and felt much better. Can you press your work reset button too? It helps to bring along some mindfulness skills.

Exercise: Reconnecting with Your Work

Here are a few simple mindfulness skills you can bring with you to work.

Take small breaks throughout the day. Even a five-minute break three times a day to walk around or close your eyes at your desk will help a great deal. If you can go outside for a breath of fresh air or a bit of sunlight, all the better.

Offer a colleague or coworker words of encouragement. Giving a compliment or offering words of encouragement goes a long way toward improving your connections with others. This week offer a coworker a kind word of appreciation. Make someone else's day!

Bring something from home that inspires you. Create a space, with a photo, a plant, or a colorful lamp, that helps you feel connected with your healthy self at work. Bring something into your space from a time when you were feeling especially good, which will remind you of moments of joy.

Start to notice feeling better at work. Notice when you have better interactions with others. Do a few extra small tasks to make the workplace function better. You will feel restored, and the days will go smoother. Give yourself kudos for small improvements. Terrific!

Organize your day so you can exercise before or after work. You may feel better when you can squeeze in a workout before work or if you plan for a workout after work. Exercising is part of a healthy recovery. Now is the time to look at your schedule to give yourself permission to add exercise back into your week.

Reconnect to your goals at work. While at your current job, take a few minutes to breathe and reflect on how you are contributing to your personal goals. Also reflect on how you are contributing to the goals of the company. Connect with your breath here, be in the present moment, and settle down. Very good!

Practice one or two of these reconnecting skills each day. Remember to think of work as a creative and energizing part of your recovery. Work with a renewed sense of purpose to enhance your personal healing.

Affirmations for Work as Recovery

We recommend you say these affirmations out loud throughout the day to connect with your intention of a mindful recovery. We also recommend you type one affirmation into your smartphone each morning as a reminder to use it three to five times daily. You can download a printable copy of these affirmations at the website for this book: http://www.newharbinger.com/40705.

Monday: *Today I look forward to bringing my best self to work.*

Tuesday: *I enjoy working and helping someone else have a good workday.*

Wednesday: *My work is my contribution to the world.*

Thursday: *Taking care of myself through my work is important to me.*

Friday: *Today I do one thing to make my work environment pleasant.*

Saturday: *I feel a sense of community and connect with other workers today.*

Sunday: *It feels great to focus on my work goals and dreams.*

SECTION 11

Sustaining Joyful Recovery

49

Recovering Each Day

Maybe happiness is this: not feeling like you should be elsewhere,
doing something else, being someone else.

—**Isaac Asimov**

It's not all going to get fixed at once. In recovery, sometimes you will feel impatient and frustrated. At other times, you might be surprised at how well your day is going. The idea of wanting things to be better right away is common. We are reminding you that you will not be able to fix everything overnight. As you move through your recovery, other things—your relationships, your job, your family, your friends, your mood, your legal issues, your physical health, your finances, and your spiritual disconnection—will need time to recover too. Instead of trying to get everything in order in one day, entertain the idea of *recovering a bit each day*. Having success in small accomplishments will feel good. Life in recovery is layered. Just as one layer begins to feel better, you'll notice another layer that needs your attention. This is as normal as it gets. To mindfully connect with your day-to-day healing, we want to introduce you to five practices that spell out DAILY. Focusing on DAILY will boost how you feel as you experience the rhythm of your recovering day.

D: Do a positive action each day. These positive actions could be emotional, physical, or spiritual. Emotionally, reconnect with how you are feeling in the moment, and continue to practice letting go of negativity. Physically, check in with your body, do some movement, exercise, or stretch some time in your day. Spiritually, plan to attend a recovery meeting, go to church or temple, meet up with your sponsor, or grab a bite to eat with a supportive friend.

A: Adjust your attitude. You'll feel a lot better if you scale down your expectations and release the need for everything to be perfect. Even a small adjustment in your attitude will have a big impact. The most powerful way to adjust your attitude is to *tap into gratitude* for yourself and others.

I: Invite quiet. You may find yourself running dangerously low on energy most of the time. Recovery is asking for some time that is *not busy.* This may mean finding a tranquil place to sit for a few minutes, taking a brief walk in nature, or just noticing a moment of silence.

L: Lie down. Give your recovery a few moments of lying down with your eyes closed. Even five to ten minutes of lying down will help you recharge for the rest of the day. When you are lying down, notice your thoughts and let them go.

Y: Younger self. Sometimes you may feel that your needs are not getting met. We'd like you to notice what your younger self might need, and offer it to yourself now. Your younger self might need a few words of encouragement, might need a cry, might need to play, or might need a special treat. Give support, encouragement, and affection to your younger self. Say to yourself, *I am where I need to be. I appreciate the journey I am on.*

There is a rhythm to your recovery, and it changes from day to day. When you pay attention to your daily experiences and make small adjustments, you are in the flow of recovering each day. One way to slow down and notice all the parts is to mindfully listen to a song. Try this next exercise and listen for your recovery.

Exercise: Listening Mindfully

This is a mindful-listening exercise. Listening with awareness allows you to slow down and notice the tempo of a song. Just like in recovery, the song doesn't come at you all at once. Music is also layered and textured.

Choose one song or a piece of music that you really enjoy. It could be jazz, classical, New Age, funk, folk-pop, rock, or country. Allow yourself ten minutes for this deep-listening exercise to unfold. Find a quiet place to listen with few interruptions, and turn off your phone's ringer. Sit comfortably. Play the music with mindful awareness of each instrument—guitar, drums, piano, saxophone—or whatever you hear. Notice the vocals: listen for the change in tone, volume, and pitch. Pay attention to the space in between the music. Notice how the song ends. And notice any emotions and images that you experienced during the song.

You have just experienced the healing art of mindful listening.

Affirmations for Recovering Each Day

We recommend you say these affirmations out loud throughout the day to connect with your intention of a mindful recovery. We also recommend you type one affirmation into your smartphone each morning as a reminder to use it three to five times daily. You can download a printable copy of these affirmations at the website for this book: http://www.newharbinger.com/40705.

Monday: *Everything I need in my recovery is within reach today.*

Tuesday: *I enjoy the simple blessings of my recovery throughout the day.*

Wednesday: *Even in stressful situations, I can find my inner strength.*

Thursday: *Today my thoughts and emotions are in line with my healing.*

Friday: *I add small moments of quiet reflection in my day.*

Saturday: *I offer myself kindness; I offer others empathy.*

Sunday: *My respect for my recovery journey begins first thing in the morning.*

50

Playful Recovery

A good laugh heals a lot of hurts.

—Madeleine L'Engle

Maybe it sounds ridiculous, but in this life you have got to find a way to *play.*

Kids have an unbelievable talent for play. My (Julie's) son, at two and a half, will spot a pint-sized person from across a crowded restaurant and announce, "I want to go play." His brother, ten months, finds play in a spoon or a packet of sugar. He covers his head with a napkin. *Peekaboo.*

It's just so natural for kids. Play seems to happen for children as easily as breathing. You could say it's easy for kids to play because they don't have bills to pay or they don't have concerns about their health or they don't have regrets weighing on their shoulders like adults do. It's a way of saying that grown-ups can't play. If you are thinking this way, you are telling yourself that you are somehow disqualified from what's best in this life. You have let yourself believe that bills to pay, health concerns, or a painful past means you must be deprived of joy. Nonsense. We suggest you let go of that belief system and fast, just as we suggest you let go of your bowling ball before you go for a swim. The capacity for play is inside you as much as it is inside a child. Because the child you were is in there, too.

This particular part of you might feel really stuck. It is possible your inner child is in a lot of pain. Maybe she had to grow up too fast and never felt like a kid at all. Maybe he is carrying a lot of hurt. Maybe your inner child seems to need some tenderness more than anything else. That may be true, and it is definitely worthwhile to give your inner kid some love. But a bit of silliness will go a long way too. Your inner child really wants to play. He might not be sure how it's going to look. Or she might be scared to ask a friend to play. Or he might pretend he thinks playing is just stupid. Or she might say she is too tired to play. But then he will get you to eat an entire bag of potato chips in front of the TV, or she will get you to spend three hours on the Internet, clicking from place to place. Call it unwinding or keeping yourself entertained. Your inner kiddo is desperate for some fun.

"I hung out with my son the other night, playing in the yard," Jason says. "It was football, I guess, but mostly we just ended up tackling each other. There was something about it…we couldn't stop laughing. It hit me all of a sudden that I was having fun. Just pure fun, like I haven't had in years. There was a time before when having fun meant getting loaded. I didn't know I could have fun anymore. When I realized it, I just felt so free."

Gift yourself with fun. Find a way to play!

Exercise 1: Adding Playfulness to Your Recovery

Using your journal, make a list of the ways you will add more play into your life. Some ideas might be having a game night and playing board games or card games with family or friends; getting a joke book and telling jokes to your friends; joining a local amateur sports league; going to an exercise class that feels silly and fun; having a dance party in your living room; doing a cartwheel if you can; rolling down a hill; sledding or ice-skating; doing cannonballs into a pool; climbing a tree; going to a local basketball court and playing pickup basketball; singing in the shower; closing your eyes and imagining you are just about anything; or playing with children, if you possibly can, games like tag, treasure hunts, guessing what the clouds are shaped like…

Now that you have a list of ideas, tap into your inner grown-up and plan your play. It would be wonderful to play spontaneously, but for starters, you may need to make the time and do some prep work to make it happen. Do some research into local sports teams or dance classes, and sign up. Contact some friends and get a game night on the calendar. Schedule a time to babysit your favorite kids. Download some new music for your dance party. Commit to one play activity a week. Put it in your planner like any other activity you are sure you are going to do, and look forward to it!

Exercise 2: Creating a Recovery Bucket List

A bucket list is a list of things you want to do before you kick the bucket. Well, now that your addiction has moved aside, there is room for so much more. Your addiction is no longer consuming so much of your time and energy, so you can channel that energy into something new. Using your journal, create a *recovery bucket list*. It's time to dream big! What amazing things do you want to see, do, and accomplish in your life? Think about places you would like to travel, adventures you would like to have, people you want to meet, creative endeavors you want to complete, and physical feats you've always wanted to try. As long as you continue your recovery, the possibilities are endless! Have fun making your bucket list, and believe wholeheartedly that you can fulfill it!

Affirmations for Playful Recovery

We recommend you say these affirmations out loud throughout the day to connect with your intention of a mindful recovery. We also recommend you type one affirmation into your smartphone each morning as a reminder to use it three to five times daily. You can download a printable copy of these affirmations at the website for this book: http://www .newharbinger.com/40705.

Monday: *I connect with the world around me when I engage in play.*

Tuesday: *Play awakens my spirit and opens my heart.*

Wednesday: *I deserve great joy in my life, and I find it when I am playful.*

Thursday: *I thrive in happy, playful recovery.*

Friday: *Today I find the playful way.*

Saturday: *My heart and mind are at ease when I let myself be silly.*

Sunday: *I make time for fun in my life.*

51

Special Occasions

Joy is being willing for things to be as they are.

—Charlotte Joko Beck

Stephanie was invited to her best friend's wedding back in their hometown. She hadn't been back home in over a year. The last time she was there, she almost got arrested for crazy behavior outside a local bar. She was panicky about going home again; most of her old friends had no idea she had stopped partying. Part of her thought she could have one drink: *Well it is a special celebration. My best friend only gets married once, right?* Stephanie needed to figure out how to go to her friend's wedding and continue in her recovery. This was brand new territory for her.

Like Stephanie, you may find special occasions to be triggers. Birthdays, anniversaries, holidays, graduations, weddings, getting a new job, buying a new home, and other special occasions are wonderful reasons to celebrate, but chances are you celebrated these happy occasions in the past with substances. You may find yourself slipping into old ways of thinking when the next special occasion comes up. As a result, discovering new ways to celebrate is an important part of your recovery. It may feel like a loss to realize that you won't be partying like you used to. You might be asking yourself: *Will I ever have any fun again? Will others think I am boring? Will I get invited anywhere again?* A new way of celebrating without your addictive behavior will indeed feel strange at first. That is why we have developed DECIDE to help you remember to make six simple choices as you get ready for your next special occasion.

D: Decline. There may be times when you will have to politely decline an invitation, especially when events take place at bars or in homes with friends who you used to party with. Declining may also be useful if you are in early recovery. Of course, you cannot avoid social celebrations forever. Declining is a short-term option as you continue to develop new skills.

E: Early. If you decide to attend the event, there may be times you will need to leave early. Leaving early allows you to take care of yourself. Let those in charge of the celebration know that you will be leaving early, and thank them for inviting you.

C: Carry your own beverages. If you have overused alcohol, we recommend you always have a nonalcoholic drink in your hand throughout any celebration. If you are offered a drink, politely smile and point to the nonalcoholic drink in your hand.

I: Invite a friend. Take a sober friend along with you. We cannot overstate how important having a friend with you will be for your recovery. That friend will be your support if you have an urge to use. Sometimes it helps to have a sign or a word that alerts your friend that you are having a tough time.

D: Dial the phone. Plan to call a support person or sponsor at a designated time during the event, whether you are triggered to use or not. Use the alert on your phone to remind you. Having a set time to talk to a trusted person has a way of calming you down so that you can enjoy the party.

E: Evaluate. Review how you handled yourself before, during, and after a big celebration. What went well? What would you like to change for the next time? This is a way for you to feel confident in your ability and will help you prepare for your next celebration. You can go to a meeting before or after an event (even if the event is out of state). There are even online meetings for you.

The next time you are invited to a special occasion or you have one of your own, decide how you will reconnect with your recovery. Stephanie decided to go to a meeting before her friend's wedding. She also put an alert in her phone to call her sponsor at the halfway mark of the celebration. And she decided to have a nonalcoholic drink in her hand all evening. She connected with her best friend and was pleasantly surprised at what a good time she had.

Audio for the next meditation exercise is available at http://www .newharbinger.com/40705.

Exercise: Visualizing Special Occasions

The next time you are invited to a special event, find a quiet place and allow yourself ten minutes in which to visualize a new level of self-awareness. Visualize the upcoming special occasion, whether it is a birthday party, a graduation, a wedding, an anniversary, or a holiday event. Picture the location, the decorations, who might attend, the food being served, and the drinks available. Imagine what you will wear. Next, imagine how you will feel and what you will say when you arrive. Imagine who will come with you and how the two of you will interact. Inhale, and as you exhale, repeat this phrase to yourself: *Peace, harmony, well-being.* Good. Again, breathe and repeat the same phrase. Nice. One more time, breathe and repeat the phrase. Spend a few minutes here. When you are ready, open your eyes and return to your surroundings. You have just filled the upcoming event with a sense of calm and personal well-being. You have what you need to experience special occasions in a new and healthy way!

Affirmations for Special Occasions

We recommend you say these affirmations out loud throughout the day to connect with your intention of a mindful recovery. We also recommend you type one affirmation into your smartphone each morning as a reminder to use it three to five times daily. You can download a printable copy of these affirmations at the website for this book: http://www .newharbinger.com/40705.

Monday: *Out of respect for my recovery, I take time to plan for an upcoming special occasion.*

Tuesday: *I make healthy decisions about how I interact with others at a special event.*

Wednesday: *Today I acknowledge that I may decline an invitation, and I communicate in a thoughtful way to the person who invited me.*

Thursday: *Self-confidence in social situations has a sacred place in my recovery.*

Friday: *I enjoy special occasions with others in a new way.*

Saturday: *The flow of recovery allows me to prepare for events by embracing my support system.*

Sunday: *I return to kindness and compassion if I get uncomfortable at a special occasion.*

52

Maintaining Recovery Over Time

My destination is no longer a place, rather a new way of seeing.

—Marcel Proust

There is an old Native American tale about a grandfather and his grandson. The grandfather tells his grandson that there are two wolves always doing battle inside of him.

"One of the wolves is light and love," the grandfather says. "He is health and happiness and peace. He keeps me strong."

"What about the other wolf?" the child asks.

"Oh, that wolf is full of darkness. He is sickness and heartache and pain. He is anger and fear. He is very dangerous. He tries to lead me astray at every turn."

"And they are always fighting?"

"Yes, always. But I do not mind, because I know who will win."

"Which wolf will win?" the grandson asks.

"That is easy," the grandfather answers. "It is the one that I feed."

Maintaining your recovery from addiction isn't always easy. It takes energy. It takes effort. It's up to you whether your recovery from addiction is a large or a small part of your life. You get to decide how much you invest. But the truth is that maintaining recovery over time will require your commitment and care. Good things usually do.

We won't sugarcoat things here: relapse is common. Depending on your situation, relapse can range from disruptive to deadly. The path to a joyful, peaceful, and fulfilling life is recovery, not addiction. And your best bet for staying clean is to feed your recovery wolf.

When it is time to make a decision, big or small, ask yourself which wolf you want to feed. Get your recovery wolf well fed. Get him rippling with muscles and covered in a shiny silver coat. Get your addiction wolf so skinny and frail that when he dares to lunge at you, one swift snarl from your recovery wolf will put that nasty creature back in his corner.

Your recovery wolf thrives when you connect with your community. Go to meetings (12-step, SMART Recovery, Celebrate Recovery, wherever you feel supported and close to people who *get it*). If you were in a treatment program, stay connected to its aftercare groups. Reach out to trusted others when you have a craving, a question, or one heck of a day. Reach out to a mental health professional when you are really stuck or you have a crisis. Addiction is a disease of isolation. Trying to handle all on your own what life throws at you is one way of feeding your addiction wolf. Stay close to a recovery community.

Your recovery wolf loves positive thoughts. Give him a steady diet of positive self-talk and affirmations. Feed him on regular doses of self-care. Exercise. Sleep. Eat nourishing food. Have a little fun. Have a lot of relaxation. With the stress of daily life, you have to carve out time to exhale. A minimum of one hour each day and one full day each week should be set aside for you to decompress (Bourne 2015).

Know your triggers and avoid them when you can. Be willing to move through them when you can't. Ride the wave of your cravings as smoothly as you can, and remember they are always temporary. Don't be afraid of cravings or any other feelings. Experience the deep wisdom of knowing that your feelings won't destroy you. Realize you are stronger than you know.

Practice your meditations regularly, and revisit them whenever you need a boost. Better yet, practice them regularly to prevent your stressors from bringing you down. Maybe you will add in chanting or prayers, join a spiritual community (a church or temple, a meditation group, or a Buddhist center), or take trainings on meditation and mindfulness. Keep learning. Keep finding what fulfills you on that deep spiritual level.

224

You have choices about what you feed in your life. To maintain your recovery from addiction, make conscious choices about how you live your life from day to day and moment to moment. Your devotion to recovery is bound to ebb and flow. You're human. Your life, and whatever you put into it, is your very own. We hope that you know you deserve good things. You are worth every gift you can give to yourself. Keep giving yourself these gifts and keep recovering!

Exercise: Claiming Your Recovery Space

One way to commit to your recovery is to physically create a space that belongs to your recovery. For this exercise, you will need to set aside a significant period of time to imagine and create your space. How long it takes will depend on what you choose to do. You could buy some weights and a punching bag and make a gym in your garage; turn a spare room into a meditation room; plant a garden or arrange some potted plants outside, where you can go to feel calm and grounded; arrange affirmations or prayers in an area of your kitchen, where you can recite them while you cook for yourself; buy and stack your favorite books for morning meditation next to your bed with a scented candle; clean your bathroom and decorate it to create a peaceful retreat; buy a small sculpture and set of meditation chimes and arrange these in the corner of your bedroom or outdoor space; choose a corner in your house as your journaling space, with a comfortable chair and a jar of fresh pens; or turn a part of your bedroom into your yoga space with a mat and relaxing music. The possibilities here are endless, even if it feels like you don't have a lot of room.

A garage, a shed, or even a closet can become your own recovery space. It is easy to feel like there isn't enough room in your life for recovery behaviors, just as it may seem like there isn't enough room in your house. That's why this exercise is so meaningful. Think creatively, rearrange a few things, and claim your space!

Affirmations for Maintaining Recovery Over Time

We recommend you say these affirmations out loud throughout the day to connect with your intention of a mindful recovery. We also recommend you type one affirmation into your smartphone each morning as a reminder to use it three to five times daily. You can download a printable copy of these affirmations at the website for this book: http://www .newharbinger.com/40705.

Monday: *I choose to feed my recovery wolf today.*

Tuesday: *It isn't always easy to maintain recovery, but I know it is worth my time.*

Wednesday: *I make decisions, moment to moment, that reflect my commitment to recovery.*

Thursday: *I value my recovery and make recovery a priority.*

Friday: *I treat myself well by engaging in self-care.*

Saturday: *Whatever I put into my recovery, I will get back tenfold.*

Sunday: *I deserve all the gifts of recovery.*

Resources for the Road

Congratulations for opening the gift of this book and reconnecting with your healthy recovery. Now you get to build on what you have accomplished. Here are some resources you can access to continue your recovery journey. We recommend you either delve into a topic that already interests you or choose a topic that is new to you. Developing a resource library is an excellent way to keep the agreement you have made with yourself to engage in a resilient recovery life.

Beginning Your Mindful Recovery

Chödrön, P. *How to Meditate: A Practical Guide to Making Friends with Your Mind*. Louisville, CO: Sounds True, 2013.

Goldstein, J. *Mindfulness: A Practical Guide to Awakening*. Reprint ed. Louisville, CO: Sounds True, 2016.

Griffin, K. *Recovering Joy: A Mindful Life After Addiction*. Louisville, CO: Sounds True, 2015.

Kornfield, J. *No Time Like the Present: Finding Freedom, Love, and Joy Right Where You Are*. New York: Atria Books, 2017.

Emotions

Cullen, M., and G. B. Pons. *The Mindfulness-Based Emotional Balance Workbook: An Eight-Week Program for Improved Emotion Regulation and Resilience*. Oakland, CA: New Harbinger Publications, 2015.

Epstein, M. *Advice Not Given: A Guide to Getting Over Yourself*. New York: Penguin Press, 2018.

McKay, M., M. Skeen, and P. Fanning. *The CBT Anxiety Solution Workbook: A Breakthrough Treatment for Overcoming Fear, Worry, and Panic*. Oakland, CA: New Harbinger Publications, 2017.

Nhat Hahn, T. *Fear: Essential Wisdom for Getting Through the Storm*. Reprint ed. New York: HarperOne, 2014.

Orloff, J. *The Empath's Survival Guide: Life Strategies for Sensitive People*. Louisville, CO: Sounds True, 2017.

Strosahl, K. D., and P. J. Robinson. *The Mindfulness and Acceptance Workbook for Depression: Using Acceptance and Commitment Therapy to Move Through Depression and Create a Life Worth Living*. 2nd ed. Oakland, CA: New Harbinger Publications, 2017.

Especially Strong Emotions

Hone, L. *Resilient Grieving: Finding Strength and Embracing Life After a Loss Changes Everything*. New York: The Experiment, 2017.

Kolts, R. *The Compassionate-Mind Guide to Managing Your Anger: Using Compassion-Focused Therapy to Calm Your Rage and Heal Your Relationships*. Oakland, CA: New Harbinger Publications, 2012.

Najavits, L. *Recovery from Trauma, Addiction, or Both: Strategies for Finding Your Best Self*. New York: Guilford Press, 2017.

Rendon, J. *Upside: The New Science of Post-Traumatic Growth*. Reprint ed. New York: Touchstone, 2015.

Sandberg, S., and A. Grant. *Option B: Facing Adversity, Building Resilience, and Finding Joy*. New York: Knopf, 2017.

Van der Kolk, B. *The Body Keeps the Score: Brain, Mind, and Body in the Healing of Trauma*. Reprint ed. New York: Penguin Books, 2015.

Winch, G. *Emotional First Aid: Healing Rejection, Guilt, Failure, and Other Everyday Hurts*. Reprint ed. New York: Penguin Group, 2014.

Thoughts

Amen, D. G., and T. Amen. *The Brain Warrior's Way: Ignite Your Energy and Focus, Attack Illness and Aging, Transform Pain into Purpose.* New York: Berkley Books, 2016.

Breuning, L. G. *The Science of Positivity: Stop Negative Thought Patterns by Changing Your Brain Chemistry.* New York: Adams Media, 2016.

Winston, S. M., and M. N. Seif. *Overcoming Unwanted Intrusive Thoughts: A CBT-Based Guide to Getting over Frightening, Obsessive, or Disturbing Thoughts.* Oakland, CA: New Harbinger Publications, 2017.

Cravings and Triggers

Johnson, A., and M. Howard. *The Little Book of Big Change: The No-Willpower Approach to Breaking Any Habit.* Oakland, CA: New Harbinger Publications, 2016.

Spickard, A. W., Jr., J. Butler, and B. Thompson. *The Craving Brain: Science, Spirituality and the Road to Recovery.* CreateSpace Independent Publishing Platform, 2016.

Szalavitz, M. *Unbroken Brain. A Revolutionary New Way of Understanding Addiction.* New York. St. Martin Press, 2016.

Williams, R. E., and J. S. Kraft. *The Mindfulness Workbook for Addiction: A Guide to Coping with the Grief, Stress, and Anger That Trigger Addictive Behaviors.* Oakland, CA: New Harbinger Publications, 2012.

Mindfulness Skills and Stress Relief

Byrne, H. G. *The Here-and-Now Habit: How Mindfulness Can Help You Break Unhealthy Habits Once and for All.* Oakland, CA: New Harbinger Publications, 2016.

Farrarons, E. *The Mindfulness Coloring Book: Anti-Stress Art Therapy for Busy People.* New York: The Experiment, 2015.

Foster, J. *The Deepest Acceptance: Radical Awakening in Ordinary Life.* Louisville, CO: Sounds True, 2012.

Greenberg, M. *The Stress-Proof Brain: Master Your Emotional Response to Stress Using Mindfulness and Neuroplasticity.* Oakland, CA: New Harbinger Publications, 2017.

Kondo, M. *The Life-Changing Magic of Tidying Up: The Japanese Art of Decluttering and Organizing.* Berkeley, CA: Ten Speed Press, 2014.

Cultivating and Improving Relationships

Barnett, R. *Addict in the House: A No-Nonsense Family Guide Through Addiction and Recovery.* Oakland, CA: New Harbinger Publications, 2016.

Fischer, J. B., and S. Kindell. *The Two Truths About Love: The Art and Wisdom of Extraordinary Relationships.* Oakland, CA: New Harbinger Publications, 2013.

Hamilton, D. M. *The Zen of You and Me: A Guide to Getting Along with Just About Anyone.* Boulder, CO: Shambhala Publications, 2017.

Nhat Hahn, T. *The Art of Communicating.* Reprint ed. New York: HarperOne, 2014.

Rye, M. S., and C. D. Moore. *The Divorce Recovery Workbook: How to Heal from Anger, Hurt, and Resentment and Build the Life You Want.* Oakland, CA: New Harbinger Publications, 2015.

Salzberg, S. *Real Love: The Art of Mindful Connection.* New York: Flatiron Books, 2017.

Vanzant, I. *Forgiveness: 21 Days to Forgive Everyone for Everything.* 2nd ed. Carlsbad, CA: Smiley Books, 2017.

Willard, C. *Growing Up Mindful: Essential Practices to Help Children, Teens, and Families Find Balance, Calm, and Resilience.* Louisville, CO: Sounds True, 2016.

Bonding with Your Body: Food

Korn, L. *The Good Mood Kitchen: Simple Recipes and Nutrition Tips for Emotional Balance*. New York: Norton, 2017.

Price-Kellogg, L., and K. Taylor. *For the Love of Food and Yoga: A Celebration of Mindful Eating and Being*. New York: Skyhorse Publishing, 2015.

Scritchfield, R. *Body Kindness: Transform Your Health from the Inside Out—and Never Say Diet Again*. New York: Workman Publishing, 2016.

Simpkins, K. *52 Ways to Love Your Body*. Oakland, CA: New Harbinger Publications, 2016.

Tribole, E., and E. Resch. *The Intuitive Eating Workbook: Ten Principles for Nourishing a Healthy Relationship with Food*. Oakland, CA: New Harbinger Publications, 2017.

William, A. *Medical Medium Life-Changing Foods: Save Yourself and the Ones You Love with the Hidden Healing Powers of Fruits and Vegetables*. Carlsbad, CA: Hay House, 2016.

Bonding with Your Body: Yoga

Abel, R. Jr. *The Eye Care Revolution: Prevent and Reverse Common Vision Problems*. Revised and updated ed. New York: Kensington, 2014.

Baptiste, B. *Perfectly Imperfect: The Art and Soul of Yoga Practice*. Carlsbad, CA: Hay House, 2016.

Carson, K., and C. Krucoff. *Relax into Yoga for Seniors: A Six-Week Program for Strength, Balance, Flexibility, and Pain Relief*. Oakland, CA: New Harbinger Publications, 2016.

Chase, S. *Yoga and the Pursuit of Happiness: A Guide to Finding Joy in Unexpected Places*. Oakland, CA: New Harbinger Publications, 2016.

Dale, C. *Subtle Energy Techniques (Cyndi Dale's Essential Energy Library)*. Woodbury, MN: Llewellyn, 2017.

Bonding with Your Body: Sleep

Black, A. *Mindfulness and Sleep: How to Improve Your Sleep Quality Through Practicing Mindfulness*. New York: CICO Books, 2018.

Carney, C. E., and R. Manber. *Goodnight Mind: Turn Off Your Noisy Thoughts and Get a Good Night's Sleep*. Oakland, CA: New Harbinger Publications, 2013.

Ehrnstrom, C., and A. L. Brosse. *End the Insomnia Struggle: A Step-by-Step Guide to Help You Get to Sleep and Stay Asleep*. Oakland, CA: New Harbinger Publications, 2016.

National Sleep Foundation. 2017. https://sleepfoundation.org.

Values and Self-Worth

Aarssen, C. *Real Life Organizing: Clean and Clutter-Free in 15 Minutes a Day*. Miami: Mango Publishing Group, 2017.

DeSilver, A. F. *Writing as a Path to Awakening: A Year to Becoming an Excellent Writer and Living an Awakened Life*. Louisville, CO: Sounds True, 2017.

Desmond, T. *The Self-Compassion Skills Workbook: A 14-Day Plan to Transform Your Relationship with Yourself*. New York: Norton, 2017.

DeYoe, J. K. *Mindful Money: Simple Practices for Reaching Your Financial Goals and Increasing Your Happiness Dividend*. San Francisco: New World Library, 2017.

Gilbert, E. *Big Magic: Creative Living Beyond Fear*. Reprint ed. New York: Riverhead Books, 2016.

Goins, J. *The Art of Work: A Proven Path to Discovering What You Were Meant to Do*. Nashville: Thomas Nelson, 2015.

Kaplan, J. *The Gratitude Diaries: How a Year Looking on the Bright Side Can Transform Your Life*. Reprint ed. New York: Dutton, 2016.

Neff, K. *Self-Compassion: The Proven Power of Being Kind to Yourself*. Reprint ed. New York: HarperCollins, 2015.

Newcomb, S. *Loaded: Money, Psychology, and How to Get Ahead Without Leaving Your Values Behind*. Hoboken, NJ: Wiley, 2016.

Richardson, K. L. *What Your Clutter Is Trying to Tell You: Uncover the Message in the Mess and Reclaim Your Life*. Carlsbad, CA: Hay House, 2017.

Simon, T. ed. *The Self-Acceptance Project: How to Be Kind and Compassionate Toward Yourself in Any Situation*. Louisville, CO: Sounds True, 2016.

Sustaining Joyful Recovery

Andrews McMeel Publishing. *Insight from the Dalai Lama 2018 Day-to-Day Calendar*. Kansas City, MO: Andrews McMeel, 2017.

Bernie, J. *The Unbelievable Happiness of What Is: Beyond Belief to Love, Fulfillment, and Spiritual Awakening*. Oakland, CA: New Harbinger Publications, 2017.

Bernstein, S., and A. Harvey. *Play Life More Beautifully: Reflections on Music, Friendship and Creativity*. Carlsbad, CA: Hay House, 2017.

Bookbinder, D. *Paths to Wholeness: Fifty-Two Flower Mandalas*. BookBaby, 2016.

Bradley Hagerty, B. *Life Reimagined: The Science, Art, and Opportunity of Midlife*. New York, NY: Riverhead Books, 2016.

Daywalt, D., and O. Jeffers. *The Day the Crayons Quit*. New York: Philomel Books, 2013.

Greenland, S. K. *Mindful Games: Sharing Mindfulness and Meditation with Children, Teens, and Families*. Boulder, CO: Shambhala Publications, 2016.

Kiloby, S. *Natural Rest for Addiction: A Radical Approach to Recovery Through Mindfulness and Awareness.* Oakland, CA: New Harbinger Publications, 2017.

Nepo, M. *The One Life We're Given: Finding the Wisdom That Waits in Your Heart.* Reprint ed. New York: Atria Books, 2017.

Sadhguru. *Inner Engineering: A Yogi's Guide to Joy.* New York: Spiegel and Grau, 2016.

Schiller, D. *Zen Page-a-Day Calendar.* New York: Workman Publishing, 2017.

References

Armstrong, L. E., M. S. Ganio, D. J. Casa, E. C. Lee, B. P. McDermott, J. F. Klau, L. Jimenez, L. Le Bellego, E. Chevillotte, and H. R. Lieberman. 2011. "Mild Dehydration Affects Mood in Healthy Young Women." *The Journal of Nutrition* 142(2): 382–88.

Bays, J. C. 2009. *Mindful Eating: A Guide to Rediscovering a Healthy and Joyful Relationship with Food.* Boston: Shambhala Publications.

Bourne, E. J. 2015. *The Anxiety and Phobia Workbook.* 6th ed. Oakland, CA: New Harbinger Publications.

Bowen, S., N. Chawla, and G. A. Marlatt. 2010. *Mindfulness-Based Relapse Prevention for Addictive Behaviors: A Clinician's Guide.* New York: Guilford Press.

Burns, D. 2008. *Feeling Good: The New Mood Therapy.* Reprint ed. New York: Harper Publishing.

Davis, M., E. R. Eshelman, E. R., and M. McKay. 2008. *The Relaxation and Stress Reduction Workbook.* 6th ed. Oakland, CA: New Harbinger.

Flores, P. J. 2004. *Addiction as an Attachment Disorder.* Lanham, MD: Jason Aronson Publishing.

Gandhi, M. K. 1993. *An Autobiography: The Story of My Experiments with Truth.* Translated by M. Desai. Boston: Beacon Press.

Ganio, M. S., L. E. Armstrong, D. J. Casa, B. P. McDermott, E. C. Lee, L. M. Yamamoto, S. Marzano, R. M. Lopez, L. Jimenez, L. Le Bellego, E. Chevillotte, and H. R. Lieberman. 2011. "Mild Dehydration Impairs Cognitive Performance and Mood of Men." *British Journal of Nutrition* 106(10): 1535–43.

Gotlink, R. A., P. Chu, J. J. V. Busschbach, H. Benson, G. L. Fricchione, and M. G. M. Hunink. 2015. "Standardised Mindfulness-Based Interventions in Healthcare: An Overview of Systematic Reviews and Meta-Analyses of RCTs." *PLoS ONE* 10(4): e0124344.

Hölzel, B. K., S. W. Lazar, T. Gard, Z. Schuman-Olivier, D. R. Vago, and U. Ott. 2011. "How Does Mindfulness Meditation Work? Proposing Mechanisms of Action from a Conceptual and Neural Perspective." *Perspectives on Psychological Science* 6(6): 537–59.

Jacobson, E. 1978. *You Must Relax: Practical Methods for Reducing the Tensions of Modern Living.* 5th revised and enlarged ed. New York: McGraw-Hill.

Kabat-Zinn, J. 2013. *Full Catastrophe Living: Using the Wisdom of Your Body and Mind to Face Stress, Pain, and Illness.* Revised and updated ed. New York: Bantam.

Kaplan, K. A., J. McQuaid, C. Primich, and N. Rosenlicht. 2014. "An Evidence-Based Review of Insomnia Treatment in Early Recovery." *Journal of Addiction Medicine* 8(6): 389–94.

Lerner, H. 2014. *Dance of Anger: A Woman's Guide to Changing the Patterns of Intimate Relationships.* Reprint ed. New York: William Morrow.

McCauley, J. L., T. Killeen, D. F. Gros, K. T. Brady, and S. E. Back. 2012. "Posttraumatic Stress Disorder and Co-Occurring Substance Use Disorders: Advances in Assessment and Treatment." *Clinical Psychology: Science and Practice (New York)* 19(3): 283–304.

Najavits, L. M. 2001. *Seeking Safety: A Treatment Manual for PTSD and Substance Abuse.* New York: Guilford Press.

Salzburg, S. 2002. *Lovingkindness: The Revolutionary Art of Happiness.* Boston: Shambhala Publications.

Wei, M. and J. E. Groves. 2017. *The Harvard Medical School Guide to Yoga: 8 Weeks to Strength, Awareness, and Flexibility*. Boston: Da Capo Lifelong Books.

Williams, R. E., and J. S. Kraft. 2012. *The Mindfulness Workbook for Addiction: A Guide to Coping with the Grief, Stress, and Anger That Trigger Addictive Behaviors*. Oakland, CA: New Harbinger.

Zhang, L., J. Samet, B. Caffo, & N. M. Punjabi. 2006. "Cigarette Smoking and Nocturnal Sleep Architecture." *American Journal of Epidemiology*, 164: 529-537.

Rebecca E. Williams, PhD, is an award-winning author, consultant, and clinical psychologist specializing in healthy recovery from mental illness and addiction. Her work focuses on building resilience and embracing well-being. She is associate clinical professor of psychiatry at the University of California, San Diego, and program director at the Veterans Affairs San Diego Health Care System.

Julie S. Kraft, MA, LMFT, is a licensed marriage and family therapist. She has been working in the fields of addiction and mental health since 2008. Julie is an adjunct faculty member at the University of San Diego, where she teaches systemic treatment of substance abuse. Julie has a private practice in San Diego, CA, where she works to help her clients find all the gifts that they deserve.

Williams and Kraft are coauthors of *The Mindfulness Workbook for Addiction*, which won the San Diego Book Award. Their workbook has been translated into Korean.

MORE BOOKS *from*
NEW HARBINGER PUBLICATIONS

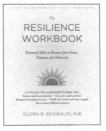

Register your **new harbinger** titles for additional benefits!

When you register your **new harbinger** title—purchased in any format, from any source—you get access to benefits like the following:

- Downloadable accessories like printable worksheets and extra content

- Instructional videos and audio files

- Information about updates, corrections, and new editions

Not every title has accessories, but we're adding new material all the time.

Access free accessories in 3 easy steps:

1. Sign in at NewHarbinger.com (or **register** to create an account).

2. Click on **register a book**. Search for your title and click the **register** button when it appears.

3. Click on the **book cover or title** to go to its details page. Click on **accessories** to view and access files.

That's all there is to it!

If you need help, visit:

NewHarbinger.com/accessories

new harbinger
CELEBRATING
40 YEARS